Truth About Food

By
Dr Aroona Reejhsinghani

HEALTH HARMONY
An imprint of
B. Jain Publishers (P) Ltd.
USA — Europe — India

TRUTH ABOUT FOOD

First Edition: 2014
1st Impression: 2014

All rights reserved. No part of this book may be reproduced, stored in a retrieval system or transmitted, in any form or by any means, mechanical, photocopying, recording or otherwise, without any prior written permission of the publisher.

© with the publisher

Published by Kuldeep Jain for

HEALTH HARMONY
An imprint of
B. JAIN PUBLISHERS (P) LTD.
1921/10, Chuna Mandi, Paharganj, New Delhi 110 055 (INDIA)
Tel.: +91-11-4567 1000 • Fax: +91-11-4567 1010
Email: info@bjain.com • Website: www.bjain.com

Printed in India by
J.J. Offset Printers

ISBN: 978-81-319-3302-2

Introduction

To maintain health, well-being and youthfulness, we should provide our bodies with the best protective foods. The right food can boost your body with nutrients to fight illness, prevent ageing and help the body to perform at its best. There are many food which have been created by nature for us. Some foods are extremely powerful in fighting diseases and so we call them 'super foods'. Each chemical in these fruits, vegetables, nuts, spices and plants contain chemicals which have a unique role to prevent disease. Some are anti-inflammatory, whilst others fight ageing, disease and regulate our hormones. When antioxidants, photochemicals and essential fatty acids like omega-3 and omega-6 were discovered by scientists, then a new class of foods was discovered which contained these super nutrients and these foods were called SUPER FOODS.

Hippocrates, the father of modern medicine said hundreds of years ago, "Let food be your medicine. Let medicine be your food." Each super food has a specific healing property. Some of the foods are so potent that they help a human being when no medicine on this earth can help him. In the bygone years, our grandmothers and their mothers depended upon food to cure them and they were cured in most cases. But today everyone depends upon a pill, quite forgetting that even a small pill can cause havoc in the body. But super foods are natural healers which have no side effects. But for the food to give health benefits to the body, you should cultivate healthy eating habits. Eat only when you are relaxed and in a happy frame of mind. Refrain from over loading your tummy. Food should be easy on your teeth, chew properly and take your time to finish your food. Drink at least ten to twelve glasses of water per day. Do not consume water during or after meals. This will dilute your digestive juices which in turn, will hamper the digestive process. Water, besides eliminating waste from the digestive tract, aids absorption of essential nutrients, regulates body temperature and also improves the quality of the skin. Water is the single most important element which helps flushing out and stopping the formation of kidney stones.

Water stops dehydration in the hot weather. Low water intake can result in muscular cramps. Water helps the body to transport and absorb the nutrients in the food we eat. It moves the nutrients through the cells ensuring that the nutrients are available to all the organs of the body. Eat the evening meal two hours before bedtime. This is because the body requires a fasting period ten to twelve hours in order to cleanse, repair and rejuvenate itself. Always eat a plate of raw vegetable salad with your meals. This way, the body will get important enzymes which will help in digesting the food by breaking them down into small particles. Do not eat junk food and highly spiced and fried food. These type of foods will harm the body. Remember, you are as healthy as the food you eat. Include spices and chillies in your daily diet. These help in cleansing the body and increasing metabolism and providing it with energy. But do not over eat the spicy food but always eat in moderation.

Always include high fibre foods in your diet because these are rich in essential nutrients, low in calories and fat. High fibre foods increase the absorption of nutrients in the body and reduces poison. Fresh vegetables, fruits and grains provide the necessary fibre. Addition to maintaining health of the body, the fibre helps in digesting food and removal of waste from the body, regulating body temperature and maintaining electrolyte balance.

Dr Aroona Reejhsinghani

Publisher's Note

The author with the rich publishing history, Dr Aroona Reejhsinghani, who also holds the record for writing the largest number of cookery books in India as entered in the Limca Book of Records, has written this book for us. Dr Aroona Reejhsinghani has 226 books, ranging from health and nutrition to cooking, in her kitty. She believes, for an overall development of our body we must treat our body with healthy foods. Nature has bestowed on us a lot of vegetables, fruits, grains, nuts and spices etc., which help us in vanquishing our day-to-day health-distress and ailments. She also reveals that there are some foods with such great medicinal values that they surpass the Medicine, in terms of curing. These natural foods have no side effects; one couldn't ask for more!

Healthy foods alone cannot combat our woes. We need to develop a healthy routine – eating or otherwise. Something, as simple and natural as water, can work wonders on our body; good skin, regulating body temperature and bidding adieu to kidney stones are the good results of drinking adequate water everyday.

This book makes you aware of the healing power latent in the spices, grains and plants etc. Use them in your daily regimen to stay healthy, forever.

Kuldeep Jain
C.E.O., B. Jain Publishers (P) Ltd.

Contents

Truth About Food .... *i*
Introduction .... *iii*
Publisher's Note .... *vii*

Chapter 1   **Plants** **1**
             • **Tulsi** **2**
             • **Tea** **8**
             • **Wheat Grass** **11**
             • **Aloe Vera** **14**
             • **Celery** **17**
             • **Spinach** **19**
             • **Neem** **21**

	• Mint	24
	• Coriander Leaves	26
Chapter 2	Spices	29
	• Nutmeg	31
	• Fenugreek Seeds and Leaves	33
	• Ginger	35
	• Garlic	38
	• Coriander Seeds	42
	• Cardamom	45
	• Asafoetida	47
	• Saffron	49
	• Thymol Seeds	52
	• Cloves	55
	• Black Pepper	58
	• Fennel	61
	• Turmeric	63
Chapter 3	Pulses and Lentils	73
	• Soya Beans	75
	• Bengal Gram	80
	• Green Gram	82
Chapter 4	Grains	85
	• Grains	85
	• Wheat	87
	• Rice	90
	• Barley	93
Chapter 5	Nuts	95
	• Almond	97
	• Cashew nuts	100

Contents   xi

- Raisin 102
- Walnuts 104
- Pistachios 106
- Ground nut 108
- Coconut 110
- Flax Seeds 112

Chapter 6   Dairy Products 113
- Milk 113
- Curd 119

Chapter 7   Honey 123
- Sugar, Jaggery and Salt 129

Chapter 8   Vegetables 133
- Broccoli and Cauliflower 136
- Beetroot 138
- Bitter Gourd 139
- Drumstick 140
- Cucumber 141
- Cabbage 142
- Carrot 144
- Chilli 146
- French Beans 147
- Gooseberry 148
- Kokum 149
- Lime 150
- Mushrooms 156
- Onions 158
- Pumpkin 160
- Sweet Potato 161

- Radish 163
- Tomato 164
- Tamarind 166
- White Gourd 168
- Fish 170

Chapter 9 Oil 173

Chapter 10 Fruits 177
- Apples 179
- Cherry 182
- Dates 184
- Grapefruit 186
- Grapes 188
- Oranges 190
- Pear 193
- Plums 195
- Peach 197
- Papaya 199
- Pomegranate 202
- Musk Melon 204
- Strawberry 205
- Sweet Lime 207
- Watermelon 208

CHAPTER I

Plants

Plants contain powerful antibiotic chemicals capable of killing powerful bacteria which can even kill a human being. Many plants like aloe vera, tulsi etc are rich in compounds that have antibacterial actions. These compounds evolved in plants give protection against pathogens which are like free radicals and which harm the body. Thomas Elaner, professor of chemical ecology of Cornell has studied the animal kingdom uses plant chemicals to cure them. He has said, "Many plant metabolites have anti-microbial potencies. For example, a bug scrapes resin from the leaves of the camphor plant and spreads it on her eggs to protect her eggs from harmful pathogens. So, the use of plants for medicinal purposes is by no means a human invention. In fact, all over the animal kingdom plants are used by them to cure themselves from all ailments.

Tulsi

The tulsi plant is of great medicinal value. Its position is unrivalled both in religious sacraments and in therapeutic value. It is said in the vedas that God does not accept any offering if it does not include tulsi. In the puranas tulsi has been described as the consort of Lord Vishnu. Lord Krishna has said in Bhagwat Gita that instead of offering costly gifts, He would be happy if He was offered a single leaf of tulsi with devotion. There is a famous story in Indian mythological. Once, Lord Krishna's wife Satyabhama weighed Him against all the legendary wealth. The scales did not balance. Then His second wife Rukmani placed a single tulsi leaf along with the wealth on the scale and the scale balanced perfectly!

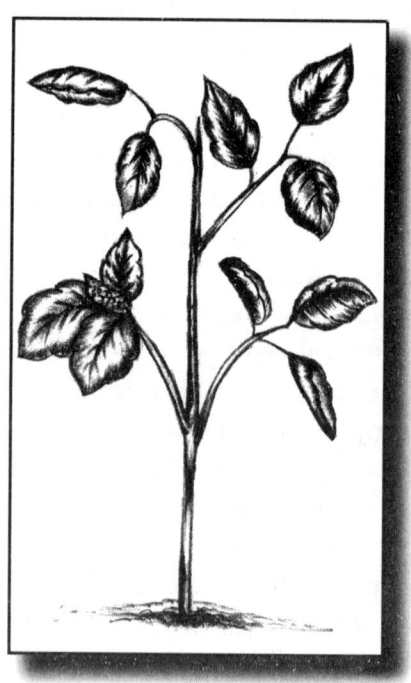

Benefits of Tulsi

The reverence towards tulsi is due to the religious beliefs of the Hindus because of its extraordinary powers of healing. Scientific research indicates that its healing powers are extremely beneficial and they not only heal but also promote health and well-being of the body. It increases the capacity to cope and adopt to changing and challenging environments and bestowing positive effects on the body and the mind.

Its anti-ageing properties improve stamina and endurance. It's an anti-oxidant who does away with free radicals strengthening the immune system. Tulsi offers heart and vascular protection and lowers blood sugar levels in diabetics, cures fever, stops bad breath, reduces nausea, vomiting and stomach cramps and protects against gastric ulcers. The essential oil in the tulsi leaves is a powerful anti-microbial. It fights germs and infections when used externally and internally.

Tulsi plant if kept in the house possesses a special capacity of killing harmful micro-organisms. The wind that carries the aroma of tulsi leaves spreads health and well being wherever it blows. If you eat even five leaves of tulsi per day, you will be protected from a large number of diseases like cough, cold, fever, stomach disorders, headache, and sore throat. Disease of the eyes and nose, itching, loss of appetite, diarrhoea, dysentery, skin diseases, sun stroke will also not happen. It also lowers fever, protects against sun stroke and ulcers, reduces dangerous blood sugar levels, improves liver functions, repels insects, gives relief from allergies and inflammations.

It also cleanses pollution in the air caused by the environmental factors like smoke and dust. Tulsi reduces stress and gives relief in many more diseases. Many more diseases are controlled by just eating tulsi. It is rightly called the 'elixir of life'.

Healing Powers of Tulsi

Fever: Juice of twenty tulsi leaves should be taken every 2 to 3 hours to bring down fever.

Mental fatigue: Add ten drops of tulsi oil in water and take a bath; tulsi oil is rich in vitamin C, carotene, calcium and phosphorus.

Ear ache: Heat a few drops of tulsi juice and put in the aching ear and you will get relief immediately.

Cough: One teaspoon of dark variety of tulsi leaf juice mixed with 1 teaspoon of honey should be taken a few times daily.

Cold: Take one teaspoon of tulsi juice. Mix with one teaspoon of honey and half a teaspoon of ginger juice. Take this thrice a day to get relief.

Pus in the ear: Boil tulsi leaf in mustard oil. Cool it a little and then put it in the affected ear to get relief.

Bad breath: Chew 25 leaves of tulsi per day with a green cardamom to be free from bad breath.

Vomiting in babies: To cure vomiting in babies, give them a drop of honey mixed with 2 drops tulsi juice. This also gives relief in cough and cold.

Abdominal pain: Take one teaspoon of tulsi juice mixed with one teaspoon of ginger juice. Warm it and drink it to get relief.

Pneumonia: Take 1 teaspoon of tulsi juice with one-fourth teaspoon pepper powder twice a day.

Flu: Mix together half teaspoon of tulsi and ginger juice, earom seeds powder along with one teaspoon of honey. Take this three times everyday to get relief.

Excessive secretion of phlegm: Grind twenty leaves of tulsi with two green cardamoms and one tablespoon of honey. Mix in one tablespoon of honey and take thrice every day to get relief.

Difficulty in breathing: Take one tablespoon of tulsi juice; mix with one teaspoon of grated jaggery to get immediate relief.

Impotency: Mix tulsi seeds with jaggery and make pea-sized pills. Take a pill thrice a day to get relief.

Boosting brain power: Boil tulsi leaves in water. Cool and drink in empty stomach in the morning. This not only improves brain power but also improves digestion.

Kidney stones: Drink tulsi juice with honey regularly to reduce kidney stones.

Worms: To get rid of worms, drink tulsi juice with equal quantity of ginger juice regularly.

Common cold: Take one tablespoon of tulsi juice with honey to cure a common cold.

Jaundice: Chew some leaves of tulsi with jaggery to get relief.

Malaria: Make dark tea with tulsi leaves, jaggery, peppercorns and lime juice. Drink it twice a day to get cured.

Typhoid: Mix together twenty tulsi leaves, ten peppercorns and half teaspoon jaggery and take once everyday to get relief.

Allergy: A paste of tulsi leaves if applied on the skin which is affected by allergic reaction will be cured in no time.

These leaves also help in cases of almost all the diseases of the skin and also remove white patches from the skin. Apply the paste of these leaves on the patches a few times daily till you are cured.

Cholesterol: To bring down cholesterol in the blood, you should daily drink tea made of tulsi leaves. When preparing the tea, boil tea leaves along with ½ tsp. grated ginger and 6 mint leaves and six tulsi leaves for 2-3 minutes. Strain, stir and sip.

Tulsi tea reduces cholesterol and hypertension. It also strengthens the immunity system, reduces stress, improves stamina, strength and endurance, helps in curing digestive problems and reduces dangerous biochemicals that bring about cancer, degenerative diseases and premature ageing.

Tulsi leaves are highly beneficial to human beauty. Make a habit of taking a teaspoon of tulsi leaf juice mixed with half teaspoon honey once everyday to get a glow in your cheeks. This juice is also very effective in removing scalp diseases and especially lice from the head. Apply tulsi juice liberally on the head before going to bed at night. Next morning wash your head with a mild shampoo and plenty of water. Do this twice a week to get an effective cure. If your baby has lice in her head, scatter the leaves on her pillow for a couple of days.

Drinking 2 teaspoons of juice of tulsi leaves in empty stomach not only rejuvenates the body but also puts a glow in it.

During the monsoons if you put a few leaves of tulsi in the drinking water it will keep you protected against all monsoon diseases.

These leaves help even when all the other medicines fail. It is rightly said, 'A tulsi leaf a day keeps all the skin ailments away'.

Tea

Tea is called the 'brew of life' since it actually lengthens our life. It's not only refreshing and energizing but it is also a great health enhancer. Tea is a natural source of fluoride bacteria in the mouth which gives rise to gum disease and dental caries.

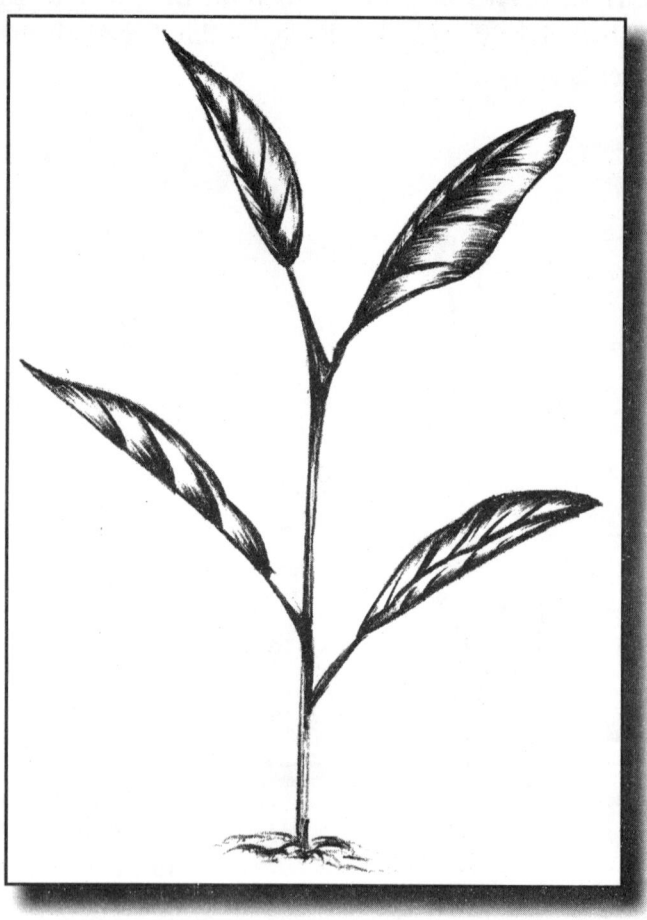

Benefits of Tea

Tea contains natural anti-oxidants which reduces the risk of heart ailments. The polyphenols in tea also help people who are victims of heart disease. It also reduces high blood cholesterol and hyper tension. Scientific studies have shown that blood cholesterol levels drops as the amount of tea consumed increases and also the blood pressure decreases significantly. The high concentration of flovanoids in tea reduces blood clotting and the deposition of cholesterol in the blood vessels.

Drinking four to five cups of tea per day reduces the risk of stroke by 69 percent.

Tea consumption may have beneficial effect in reducing cancer. Results of the most recent research published in nutrition and cancer journal indicated that tea may give protection against pancreatic and prostrate cancer.

Researchers from national centre for Toxicological Research in the United States of America extracted the flavins, polyohenola and demonstrated that they significantly inhibited the growth of human pancreatic and prostrate tumour cells. This research also indicated that tea could also have a role to play in changing the genes involved in the process of causing cancer.

Tea also helps patients suffering from prostrate cancer. This may be due to the fact that tea has a high concentration of certain antioxidants called phytochemicals which help the body fight the harmful effects of radicals.

Left-over tea leaves are very useful in preventing hair fall and they make the hair glossy and soft. Next time don't throw the used tea leaves away. Use them for washing your hair. Put the leaves in a bucket of water and boil for fifteen minutes. Remove from fire, cool, strain and use for washing the hair. Add lime juice to tea water and use it as a last rinse to provide a sheen to the hair.

Tea leaves are also very good for reviving tired eyes, mix some crushed ice with used tea leaves. Tie them up in two small pieces of cloth and put them on each eye lid for ten minutes. They will not only remove tiredness from the eyes but will also make them look brighter.

Tea leaves are an excellent remedy for treating sun burns. Dissolve four teaspoon of tea leaves in boiling water. Strain and mix with clear greasy surgical jelly and store in an airtight jar. Use when required on sunburns.

But amongst all types of tea, green tea is the richest source of anti oxidants. A cup of green tea each day, not only refreshes the body but also enhances health and stops ageing. It restricts the increase of blood cholesterol, stops dental caries, freshens the breath, lowers blood sugar levels, suppresses tumour and cancer and prevents hair fall.

To prepare green tea, put a teaspoon of green tea in a cup and fill the cup with boiling water. Cover the cup for two minutes. Strain and add a few drops of lime juice and sugar to taste and enjoy. Do not add milk.

Plant

Wheat Grass

Wheat grass juice is called the 'green gold' because this juice not only gives complete nourishment to the body but cures even incurable disease. It contains a variety of different live minerals and vitamins which are found in the blood of a healthy man.

Benefits of Wheat Grass

The juice contains vitamins A, B, E and K in large amounts. This juice contains 600 percent more vitamin B than wheat. Scientists believe that wheat grass contains Vitamin B 17 in large amounts. This vitamin is anti-cancerous in nature and therefore it helps in curing cancer.

Besides, it is the highest source of magnesium which is very essential to keep thirty enzymes in our body active.

The chlorophyll contained in the wheat grass purifies the blood and destroys hostile bacteria thriving in the intestines. The chlorophyll particles are similar to haemoglobin and therefore work as an iron element in anaemia. Dr Biiracher, a research scientist calls chlorophyll concentrated, 'sun power'. According to him, chlorophyll increases the function of liver, intestines, vascular system, lungs and bladder.

The diseases which can be cured by taking wheat grass regularly are cancer, stomach diseases, diabetes, heart disorders, gynecological diseases, premature graying of hair, impotence, asthma, parkinson's disease, insomnia, constipation, chronic cold and diseases of the eyes and the ears.

Growing Wheat Grass

To take wheat grass juice you have to grow wheat grass. Take seven small earthernware pots. Fill three-fourths of the pot with black soil and one-forth with natural manure.

Soak wheat whole night in water. Next day, tie it up in a cloth and hang it up on a nail on the wall. Sprinkle water a couple of times on the cloth. By the end of twelve hours the wheat grains will be sprouted. Everyday sow the sprouted wheat in one pot and sprinkle water on the pot every 24 hours. The wheat sown in the first pot will be of seven inches in height on the seventh day. This wheat grass should be pulled out, washed nicely and should be eaten by chewing it properly.

After sucking out the juice, the fibres should be spitted off out. If you want you can also drink its juice. After the wheat grass is removed from the pot, the soil should be dried then a small quantity of manure should be added to it before wheat is sown again.

It should be remembered that only one pot should be prepared in a day. All the seven pots should not be prepared together. The juice should be sipped in small sips in empty stomach to get the best benefit from it.

Aloe Vera

Aloe vera is a miracle plant because it has miraculous health, beauty and healing properties. This plant contains aloe vera gel which can be used both internally and externally.

A tablespoon of aloe vera gel taken in empty stomach in the morning and again in the night helps to combat a number of digestive diseases. In order to extract the gel, tear open the leaf and scrape off the sticky gel in a cup and drink it fresh twice a day.

Use it for twelve weeks. Give a break for ten days and then resume. Pregnant and nursing mothers should not consume it because this acts as a laxative.

Healing Powers of Aloe Vera

Indigestion: Aloe vera gel taken twice a day reduces acidity, heart burn and indigestion. It is an excellent remedy for combating a dry skin if applied externally.

Wounds: Any wound or cut heals properly if aloe vera gel is applied on it.

Aids: If aloe vera gel is taken internally it inhibits HIV germs and is also a nutritional support for HIV patients. An extract of mannose one of the sugars found in aloe vera, inhibits HIV 1 the virus associated with aids.

Paoisais: To heal lesions of this disease rub olive oil on the affected parts and on top rub aloe vera gel. Do these 3 to 4 times daily; also take it internally twice a day.

Arthritis: Take 2-4 tablespoons of the gel daily to relieve the pain of arthritis. This gel is also effective in curing rheumatoid arthiritis, ostoarthiritis and cancer.

Diabetes: Half teaspoon of aloe vera gel taken daily in empty stomach reduces sugar levels in 14 weeks.

Digestive tonic: Half teaspoon of aloe vera gel taken daily gives relief in constipation, ulcers, colitis and other digestive disturbances.

Burns and scalds: The immediate application of aloe vera leaf gel on burns and injuries reduces the chances infection.

Itching: Aloe vera gel is a mild anaesthetic. It also relieves itching, swelling and pain.

Aches and pains: Aloe vera gel is useful in muscle aches, pains and other joint discomforts. It is also used to treat sports injuries like sprains, strains and tendonitis.

Prickly heat and hives: Applying aloe vera gel on babies for nappy rashes and other skin infections like prickly heat, hives and insect bites gives instant relief.

Hair conditioner: The inner portion of the aloe vera skin if massaged into the hair fifteen minutes before taking head bath will make the hair shiny, healthy and dandruff free.

Sunburns: Aloe vera gel relieves pain and discomfort of sunburn. The gel acts as a barrier against the UV rays of the sun and at the same time moisturizes, conditions and nourishes the skin.

Suntan: Break an aloe vera leaf and apply the oozing gel on to the face and neck; mash after 15 minutes. This removes the tan, impurities and also gives a shine to the skin.

Aloe vera was used in ancient Egypt for beautifying the skin. It is said to hydrate, repair, calm and rejuvenate the skin both internally and externally. It also helps the skin cells to repair themselves and prevents water loss from the epidermis and increases production of collagen which keeps the skin young and tight.

Celery

Celery's medicinal properties were mentioned in the 9th century B.C. when it was mentioned by the Greek poet Homer in his epic Odyssey. The Greeks made garlands of these leaves and put them around the necks of their renowned athletes. The ancient Romans used them in food. Celery is a sister of carrots fennel, parsley and dill.

Benefits of Celery

This vegetable is an excellent source of Vitamin C. So it helps to improve the immune system because it is a rich source of antioxidants which kills free radicals. It is a rich source of potassium and sodium which are excellent for regulating the fluid balance in the body and helps the body get rid of excessive fluid and stimulates production of urine.

Celery helps in preventing cancer because its compounds prevent the free radicals from damaging the cells in the body, thus decreasing the mutation that increases the potential for cells to become cancerous. These compounds have shown to stop the growth of tumour cells. It is also a rich source of fibre. So, it is an excellent food for diabetics and also for people who are suffering from digestive disturbances.

Spinach

Spinach is called the green wonder because scientists have zeroed on at least 13 different flavonoid compounds that function as antioxidants and anti-cancer agents. These agents slow down cell division in stomach cancer cells and also help in skin cancer and breast cancer.

Benefits of Spinach

Spinach is a rich source of Vitamin K which is very important for bone health and also inducing blood clotting. Vitamin K1 activates osteocalcin the major non-collagen protein in bones. Osteocalcin has calcium molecules inside the bones.

So, if your body has less of vitamin K1, oesteocalcin levels go down and the minerals in the bones go down too giving rise to weakness and pain in the bones and joints.

Spinach contains lutian which reduces the risk of cardiovascular diseases, strokes and muscular degeneration. Spinach is an excellent food for obese people, people with diabetes and constipation.

Spinach contains chlorophyll which is a powerful insecticide. Chewing spinach leaves destroys germs in the teeth and keeps them healthy. Chlorophyll also destroys hostile bacteria in the body. Chlorophyll contains proteins and iron which gives relief in weakness and anaemia. Spinach and other greens give relief in acidity, indigestion and constipation.

Determinate Effects of Spinach

Spinach also contains a substance called purines. Excessive intake of purines can lead to health problems in some people because purines are broken down by the body to form uric acid. Excessive intake of purines can lead to excessive accumulation of uric acid and too much of this acid can give rise to gout and kidney stones.

Therefore, people who have gout or kidney stones should avoid spinach. Even otherwise this leafy vegetable should be eaten in a limited quantity only.

Neem

Neem is called the 'tree of life' because it cures practically all diseases. Neem is very dear to Indians. It enjoys a very important place in their lives. Its leaves are made into garlands along with flowers for adorning the Gods and Goddesses. Smoke from the burning leaves is wafted into the rooms to cleanse them and keep them insect free.

Benefits of Neem

Brides are given ritual bath in neem infused water to give them a clean, soft and glowing skin.

New born babies are laid on a bed of neem leaves to provide them with protective aura.

Neem oil is known to be a potent spermicide and is very effective when applied intravaginally before intercourse.

Healing Powers of Neem

Leprosy: Neem oil is very effective in treating this disease when applied externally.

Teeth cleaning: Cleaning teeth with neem twigs which not only keeps the teeth healthy and free of gum disease but also kills oral bacteria.

Digestive disturbances: The neem leaves are said to aid in digestion and stimulate the liver. So, they are known to cure jaundice, treat diseases of the lungs and help diabetics by reducing sugar in the blood.

Blood purifier: Chewing five leaves daily of neem not only purifies the blood but, improves the quality of the voices and prevents chronic diseases.

Cuts and wounds: To get quick relief, apply the neem leaf paste on them to get relief.

Itching skin: Boil neem leaves in water and take a bath with it to remove itching.

Allergies: Juice of neem leaves if taken daily helps to reduce allergies, diabetes and a variety of skin diseases.

Dandruff: A massage with neem oil every night before going to bed helps in curing dandruff.

Neem leaves are very useful for removing scars from the body caused by chickenpox. They also remove small boils and prickly heat. Boil some leaves in a bucket of water. When the water is reduced to three fourths its original quantity, cool and strain the water. Use this water to bathe and within a week you will find definite improvement in your condition.

Itching-Grind together equal quantities of neem and tulsi leaves and put to boil in oil. When a black residue settles at the bottom of the vessel, cool and bottle. Apply on the itching parts to get relief.

Diabetes: Take one cup of juice of bottle gourd. Mix with one teaspoon of tulsi leaf and neem leaf juice. Drink in empty stomach. This will not only bring down the sugar levels in the blood and urine, but also energise the body.

Take ten leaves of neem, ten tulsi leaves, ten bael leaves (a tree typical to India) and ten peppercorns. Boil in one cup of water. When it is reduced to half its quantity, drink it in empty stomach in the morning. This helps in curing borderline diabetes completely.

Mint

Greek mythology believes that mint was named after the nymph Minthe. Goddess Persephone transformed Minthe into a plant because she had a secret affair with Flades, Goddess Persephone's husband. Since he could not reverse his wife's spell, he gave Mintho such a sweet and alluring appearance and aroma that the plant was not only used in dishes but also for curing many ailments. Some are enumerated below:

Upset stomach: Boil one teaspoon green tea in one cup water, with a few mint leaves and two tablespoons of honey. Strain and sip. This not only soothes your tummy and nerves but also your throat.

Stained teeth: Powder of dried mint leaves if used regularly on the teeth will whiten and brighten them.

Acidity: Chew the mint leaves in empty stomach every morning to cure acidity.

Sore throat: In a glass of water add ½ onion, 2 cloves, 5 mint leaves, 3 peppercorns and a small piece of cinnamon stick. Boil the water till it is reduced to half its original quantity. Strain, add honey to taste, sip slowly to get relief.

Mint expels gas from the stomach. It is also useful in preventing dysentery and diarrhoea and other gastro intestinal problems.

Abdominal pain: Mix two teaspoons of mint juice with 2 teaspoons of honey and one teaspoon of lime juice. This is an excellent medicine for all types of stomach problems.

Mint contains Vitamins A and E and so it gives energy to the body and the blood vessels.

Cholera: Take 21 tablespoons each of mint, onion and lime juice. It these are mixed together and if taken in cholera, a helps the patient greatly to recover.

Ringworm: Paste of mint leaves if applied on the affected portion gives quick relief.

Coriander Leaves

Coriander leaves are a rich source of proteins, carbohydrates, calcium, phosphorous, iron and vitamins A and C. Coriander leaves are fragrant and aromatic and are commonly used in many dishes.

Since these leaves are rich in vitamin A they are very good for eyes, skin and ears.

Visual black rules and headache can be cured by taking 1 tablespoon coriander leaf juice with sugar everyday.

To stop vomiting, take 1 teaspoon coriander leaf juice every 15 minutes.

Since they remove toxins from the body they should be used liberally in the food.

To stop nose bleeding smell coriander leaf juice and apply coriander leaf paste thickly on the forehead.

To cure insomnia, mix honey and lime juice with one tablespoon coriander leaf juice and drink every night before going to bed.

CHAPTER 2

Spices

Food without spices is as unimaginable as a day without the sun. Spices give a pleasant touch to the cuisine with their aroma, pungency, flavour, taste and tang. Spices besides tickling the taste buds possess countless medicinal properties. Many of the spices like garlic, onions, chillies and ginger can inhibit seventy-five percent to hundred percent of the bacteria which are harmful to the body. Spices also help clean foods of pathogens thereby contributing towards health and longevity.

Some spices which have weak antibiotic effect become more potent when combined with other spices for example chillies, garlic, onions and cumin seeds have more potent anti-microbial effect together than a single spice.

In the hot season, when you eat spicy foods it makes the body cool by making it sweat. Spices also provide important nutrition to the body. Pungent spices are natural food preservatives which stop the growth of dangerous micro-organisms. Besides, spices stimulate the imagination and the palate with their vast ranging colours, flavours, aroma and taste.

Nutmeg

Nutmeg is a highly aromatic spice. It is used to flavour sweets, beverages, kormas, briyanies and curries. It is stimulant, culminate and astringent. It is aphrodisiac when used in pan and betel nut preparation. It gives relief in dysentery, diarrhoea, flatulence, nausea, vomiting, malaria and the early stages of leprosy. It keeps boils away, heals broken bones and helps prevent rheumatism. It also treats gastric troubles, indigestion, dysentery, vomiting and also bloating. It also helps in the treatment of arthritis, neuralgia, muscle pain and poor blood circulation. Regular consumption of this spice can give relief in joint pain and gout. In a glass of milk, add a few pinches of nutmeg and sweeten with honey. Drink this once a day to get relief

Nutmeg or (Jaiphal in Hindi) is a delicately flavoured spice. It is ground from the seeds of the nutmeg fruit. The fruit is golden yellow and resembles an apricot. It grows on a dark leafed tropical ever green tree about 30 to 60 feet in height. When ripe, the fruit loses its moisture exposing its shiny brown seeds. The seeds are covered by a fibrous material which are flattened, dried and ground into spice. From nutmeg, a volatile oil is produced for use in cases of renal and hepatic colic and for certain nervous ailments.

Nutmeg oil aids in digestion, stops vomiting, dysentery and counteracts the effects of certain poisons.

Insomnia: Nutmeg oil is rubbed on the temples before going to bed to get a sound sleep.

Alternatively, you can boil in 1 cup water 1/8th teaspoon nutmeg powder till it is reduced to half and drink before going to bed. You will be able to sleep throughout the night. Another good remedy for getting rid of sleeplessness is to soak a nutmeg in 1 cup water for 3 hours. Strain and mix in 2 cups fresh coconut water and drinking 3 to 4 times per day.

Diarrhoea: Prepare a paste of half teaspoon nutmeg and dilute in ¼ cup of milk. Add sugar and drink a few times daily to get relief.

Fever: Take 100 grams leaves of tulsi plant, 10 peppercorns and 1 nutmeg. Grind and make pea sized pills, dry in the shade. Take these pills 3-4 times each day to reduce fever.

Indigestion: Mix a pinch of nutmeg with 1 tablespoon amla juice and take 2 to 3 times each day.

Sexual pleasure: Nutmeg has the properties to prolong sexual pleasure. 1 teaspoon nutmeg powder taken with 1 tablespoon honey along with a boiled egg taken an hour before sexual intercourse helps prolong the duration of the sexual act.

Fenugreek Seeds and Leaves

It is mostly used in curry powders, curries and pickles. It is used to cure chronic flatulence, diarrhoea, dyspepsia, dropsy, enlargement of spleen and liver, rickets, gout and diabetes.

If eaten with jaggery, it gives strength to women after childbirth. It also helps to produce breast milk.

25 grams of fenugreek seeds if soaked in water and then eaten next morning in empty stomach, reduces sugar in the blood.

25 grams of powder of fenugreek seeds mixed one glass warm milk and drunk daily cures constipation in diabetic patients. Fenugreek seeds soaked in water for a few hours and ground to a paste and applied on the scalp, removes dandruff and makes hair healthy and shining. Fenugreek leaves promotes the secretion of bile they are heart friendly and help in reducing sugar in diabetics.

These leaves provide benefits the patients of dyspepsia, rheumatism, piles and worms. The leaves prevent diarrhoea, vomiting and cough.

Fenugreek seeds are useful in controlling diarrhea. One teaspoon of fenugreek seeds should be fried in one teaspoon of butter and mixed in a cup of buttermilk. This should be taken twice in a day,

Ginger

Ginger has been used for thousands of years both to spice up the food and to soothe the digestive system. Ginger alleviates the symptoms of motion sickness, helps in cough and cold and improves circulation. It is good for eyes and throat and is a great tonic for the health of the intestines for it destroys intestinal parasites.

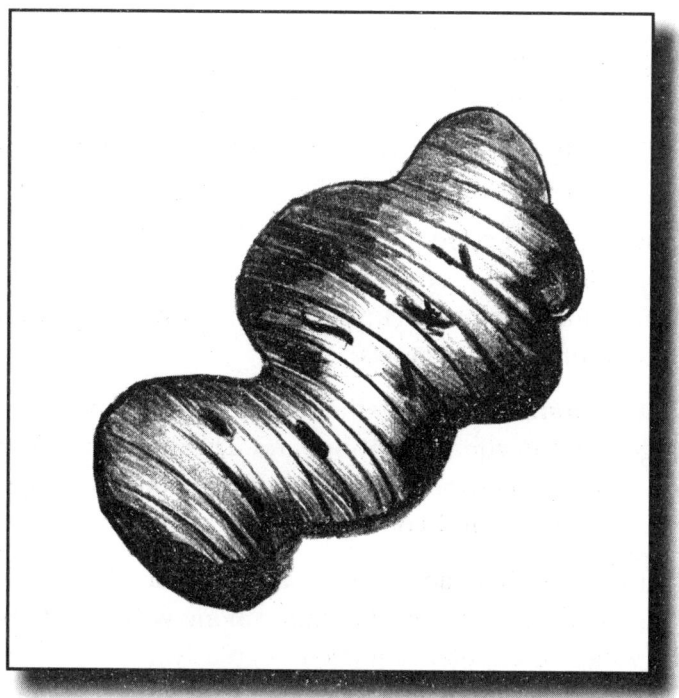

Ginger juice helps in digestion and prevents the formation of gas in the stomach. A small piece of ginger taken with a pinch of black salt half an hour before meals eliminates gastric troubles and other abdominal disorders.

It is of great help in curing cough, cold, jaundice, piles, asthma and cardiac troubles.

Some of the disease which can be cured by it are:

Indigestion: Two tablespoons of ginger juiced mixed with little black salt and one teaspoon lime juice taken before meals helps in the digestion of food.

Cancer: Ginger juice mixed with milk and taken a couple of times daily helps in reducing this disease.

Toothache: Rub a piece of ginger on the aching tooth to reduce pain.

Dry cough: Ginger eaten with black salt or ginger eaten with honey a few times daily helps in curing cough.

Vomiting: ½ teaspoon of ginger juice mixed with one teaspoon of honey, one teaspoon of lime and one teaspoon of mint juice helps in curing vomiting and also morning sickness of pregnant ladies

Gastric trouble: Mix together cumin seeds, salt, lime and ginger juice in equal quantities and dry in the sun. Powder and take one teaspoon twice daily to get relief from gastric troubles, nausea and vomiting.

Aphrodisiac: It is an excellent aphrodisiac. A mixture of ginger and honey taken at bedtime along with a half boiled egg will cure impotency if taken regularly.

Indigestion in babies: If a baby is unable to digest milk, add a few drops of ginger juice to the milk. Cough in babies can be cured by mixing a few drops of ginger juice and honey and giving it to the baby.

Cold and cough: Drink ginger tea when suffering from cold. Boil water put some grated ginger in a tea pot and pour boiling water over it. Let it stand for at least ten minutes. Sweeten with honey and drink it. Ginger is a natural remedy for nausea, morning sickness, stomach upsets and gastric troubles

Heart burn: Ginger helps strengthen the lower oesophageal sphincter, the valve that keeps the stomach acid from reversing into the oesophagus and causing a burning sensation. Make tea with fresh ginger or add to a cup of hot water, sweeten with honey and drink twice a day.

Digestive problems: Two teaspoons of ginger juice, half teaspoon lime juice and a pinch of black salt—if this is taken half an hour before meals, it improves digestion and prevents the formation of gas.

A small piece of ginger eaten with black salt dislodges phlegm and gives relief in cough and common cold.

Malignancy of the tongue: Ginger juice if taken regularly keeps malignancy of tongue away. This juice even cures cancer of the pancreas. Ginger stimulates the circulation and eases congestion in the throat and lungs. It also soothes the throat and prevents nausea. It has natural anti-inflammatory properties and it helps in cases of arthritis.

Garlic

Garlic is a member of the lily family and has been used both for cooking and medicinal purposes. For more than four thousand years, garlic as a herb had alleviated countless medicinal problems.

Some diseases where ginger is very effective in curing are:

Asthma: Grind garlic and mix with ghee and apply on the chest for curing bronchitis, asthma and cold. For headache due to cold, this mixture gives sure relief

Boils: Garlic paste mixed with little oil and turmeric powder is a sure cure for boils.

Chest cold: A baby who suffers from chest cold should be made to wear a garland of unpeeled garlic flakes. The garlic should be worn close to her chest for relief

Hypertension: Patients should eat five flakes of garlic in an empty stomach daily. This not only provides relief in hypertension but also gives relief in dizziness and insomnia which are by products of this condition.

Fast pulse: Garlic eaten in empty stomach brings down the rate of the pulse.

Stuffed nose: Inhalation of the vapours of crushed garlic removes stuffiness of the nose. If the vapours are taken at the initial stage when the cold sets in then it cures the common cold

Asthma: Boil 4 flakes of garlic in one cup milk till it is reduced to half its original quantity. Drink every night at bed time give relief to asthma patient.

Heart: It is heart healthy because it helps to break up cholesterol in the blood vessels preventing hardening of arteries which leads to heart attack. It also helps in removing toxins from the body, revitlises blood, promotes blood circulation and prevents infections from attacking the body.

If garlic is eaten regularly it stimulates the brain, heart and sexual glands, increases Vitamin B in the body which helps strengthen the nerves and tissues of the heart. It contains natural antibiotics that act against fifteen harmful bacteria in the body.

It stimulates the pituitary gland which is the director of all the glands in the body and directs the body to digest fats, starch, carbohydrates which would otherwise make the body obese.

The strong odour it emits is due to the presence of volatile oils that have remarkable medicinal value. It also contains anti-bacterial and anti-fungal properties that inhibits cancer causing genes.

It also has anti-inflammatory effect on the body. So, it is of great help in the treatment of arthritis. If taken regularly it improves the immune system and increases the life span.

The key to garlic's health giving properties is allicin. This powerful phytochemical has numerous health benefits. The allicin breaks down into a number of other compounds that act as anti-oxidants, detoxifiers, anti-cancer and anti-clotting agents.

It also contains sulphides that lowers cholesterol in the blood and keeps the heart healthy and strong. It also boosts the immune system and prevents the body from falling a victim to dangerous and incurable diseases.

To get the full benefit of garlic, take 5 flakes garlic and fry them in one tablespoon pure ghee. Mix red chillies, salt and sesame seed and grind to a paste. Eat daily to get its benefits completely. This chutney also increases the sexuality of a human being.

Garlic was used as aphrodisiac by ancient Greeks, Romans, Chinese and Japanese. This unique spice surpasses all spices in its health bestowing properties. An ancient Egyptian medical text book written in 1550 BC lists 800 diseases which can be cured with garlic. Garlic juice even when diluted to one part per 1000 parts, kills millions of deadly bacteria.

Garlic is nature's antibiotic that kills disease causing viruses and bacteria and keeping the body healthy. Garlic helps in growth of hair and makes them healthy and strong.

One tablespoon of garlic juice taken with one tablespoon of water destroys cholera germs. Garlic helps in cases of diseases like typhoid, pneumonia and paralysis.

Garlic is of great help to people who suffer from insomnia. It also helps people suffering from tuberculosis. Garlic is of great value to people who are thin because it helps in putting on weight. It also improves ones mood.

Always try to eat one or two cloves of garlic per day either in the raw form or by adding it to your food because it always does good to the body by chasing away many diseases. To reduce the strong smell of garlic in your breath, chew a cardamom or two.

Coriander Seeds

Coriander seeds are fragrant, appetizers and helps in digestion. It also is good for eyes and heart and excellent for preventing anaemia.

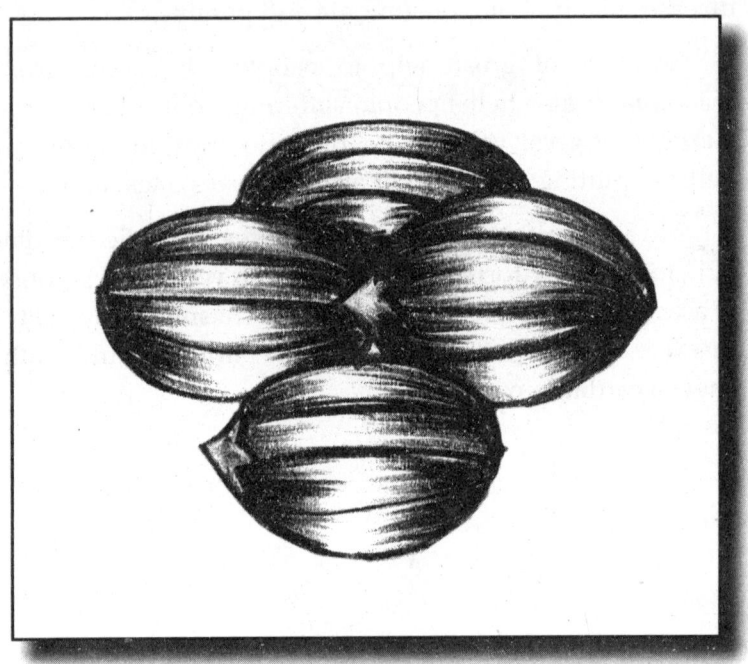

Some of the diseases which can be cured by coriander seeds are:

Body odour: Roast and grind coriander seeds to a powder. Boil half a teaspoon of this powder in a cup of water. Strain and mix a few drops of your favourite perfume and apply in your arm pits for a few minutes with a piece of cotton wool. This controls bacteria in the armpits which cause body odour. This seed contains 20 chemicals which reduces body odour.

Menstrual cycle: Boil two teaspoons of coriander seeds in two glasses of water. When it is reduced to half, mix in a few drops of vinegar. Strain and drink on the first four days of the menstrual cycle to regulate the it.

Coriander leaves are a rich source of Vitamin A and are therefore excellent for maintaining the health of the eyes, skin and hair. They also help in removing the toxins from the body. So, they should be used liberally in the food.

Palpitation: To cure this problem, soak ten grams of coriander seeds in half cup of water for a night. In the morning, grind the mixture, strain add sugar candy and drink. This also stops blood in stools.

Indigestion: To cure indigestion take fifty grams coriander seeds and mix in twenty five grams each of thymol seeds, peppercorns and black salt. Roast and powder and put in airtight bottle. Take half a teaspoon daily with water to get relief from your digestive problems.

Nose bleed: To stop nose bleeding make the patient inhale the vapours from the juice of coriander leaves and also apply the paste on the forehead of the patient.

Night discharge: To prevent this, grind together equal quantities of sugar candy and coriander seeds. Eat a teaspoon every morning and evening to get permanent relief.

For burning in the urinary tract, soak 10 grams coriander seeds and one dry amla in half cup water. Grind, strain and drink every morning. This also cures frequent thirst.

Insomnia: The best cure for this condition is to mix honey and lime juice with one tablespoon of coriander leaf juice and drinking it every night.

Visual blackout and headache: This condition can be cured by taking one tablespoon of coriander leaf juice with sugar twice everyday.

Vomiting: To cure this condition drink coriander leaf juice every fifteen minutes.

Headache: Headache due to heat can be cured by soaking one tablespoon coriander seeds with 1 dry amla in a mud vessel for a night. Grind, strain add sugar and then drink it.

Palpitation of the heart: To cure this, soak 10 grams of coriander seeds in half cup water for a night. In the morning grind the mixture, strain, add powdered sugar and drink. This also stops blood from coming in the urine.

To cure indigestion, take 50 grams of coriander seeds and mix with 25 grams each of thymol , pepper and black salt. Grind and bottle. Take half a teaspoon everyday to get relief.

To prevent night discharge, grind equal quantities of sugar and coriander seeds and store in an airtight bottle. Eat one teaspoon every morning in empty stomach.

To cure burning in the urinary tract and frequent thirst, soak 10 grams of coriander seeds in half cup water of with one dry amla. Grind, strain and drink every morning.

To prevent headaches due to heat, soak one tablespoon coriander seeds with one dry amla in an earthen vessel. Grind, strain and add powdered sugar and drink it.

Cardamom

Cardamoms are aromatic seed capsule of a reed like plant grown chiefly in the western coastal regions of India. The seeds within the pods are used for both flavouring and seasoning. The size of the pods range between 1 cm to 5 cm. The smaller sized pods are considered best for flavouring a variety of sweets and savouries. The peels of the pods are used in medicines.

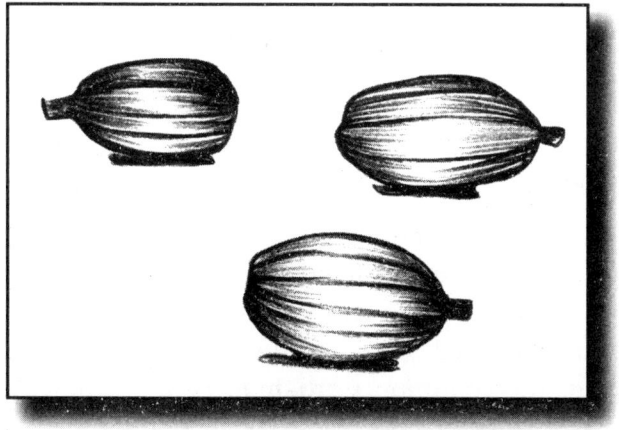

Some diseases which can be cured by Cardamom are:

Cardamoms relieve flatulence, aid digestion and stimulate the stomach to manufacture more acid which in turn improves digestion.

Cardamoms also act as mouth freshener. After food if cardamoms are chewed, they refresh the breath and remove the bad smell of strong smelling food like radish, garlic and onions.

Diarrhoea: One tablespoon of cardamom seeds roasted and powdered with four tablespoon of cumin seeds and taken in the quantity of a teaspoon with warm water twice daily is a sure cure for loose motions.

Depression: Tea made with cardamoms and sweetened with honey removes depression in a person.

Acute diarrhoea: Equal quantities of cardamom seeds, black cumin seeds and anise seeds should be roasted powdered and bottled. Half teaspoon of this powder if taken with warm water after the gap of every three hours will cure this condition.

Fever: Tulsi leaves boiled in water along with powdered cardamoms and favoured with milk and sugar taken every three hours brings down fever.

Vomiting: In a pan leaf, place 2 tablespoons pomegranate seeds and 4 small cardamoms. If this is eaten, it cures vomiting. Tulsi leaf juice mixed with powdered cardamoms, pinch of powdered cloves and sugar candy proves beneficial in curing this condition. Cardamom seeds eaten with sugar and tulsi leaves are effective in curing vomiting.

Impotence: Cardamom powder boiled in milk and sweetened with honey proves very effective in curing impotence and premature ejaculation.

Eating a cardamom with a tablespoon of honey improves the eye sight and strengthens the nervous system. Eating cardamoms over strong smelling foods like garlic and onions acts as a mouth freshener.

Large black cardamoms are usually used in curry powders and seasoning of briyanies, mutton and chicken dishes.

Asafoetida

Asafoetida (called hing in hindi) is imported from Afghanistan and Iran. Pure asafoetida is extremely pungent to the nostrils. What we use in our day to day use is the compounded variety. It is called compounded because the main product is mixed with gum Arabic and starch. The vapours of asafetida during its manufacture produce profuse watering in the eyes. So, the eyes of the workers are completely protected while they are working. Asafoetida helps in the following:

Recurrent infection of the skin: Take 50 ml of coconut oil, five flakes crushed garlic, three pieces camphor, ¼ teaspoon of asafetida and pinch of salt. Heat oil and add garlic. When the garlic turns red, mix the remaining ingredients. Cool and bottle. This oil brings down swelling and reduces burning of the skin when applied externally a few times daily.

Ear infection: Wrap a tiny piece of asafetida in a piece of cloth and keep in the affected ear to get relief. Do not force it inside.

Respiratory disorders: Mix 1/8 teaspoon of asafoetida with 2 teaspoons of honey, ¼ teaspoon of onion juice and 1 teaspoon betel leaf juice. Take three times daily to cure whooping cough, asthma and bronchitis.

Sexual dysfunctions: Fry 1/8 teaspoon of asafoetida in one teaspoon of pure ghee. Mix it with 1 teaspoon of honey and 1 teaspoon of fresh latex of the banyan tree. Take the mixture twice daily to cure impotency and premature ejaculation.

Leucorrhea: Mix one-fourth teaspoon of fried asafoetida in ½ cup goats milk and 1 tablespoon honey. Take this thrice a day for a month to be cured of this condition. This also cures painful menses, sterility and frequent abortions

Toothache: Make a paste of asafoetida and water and apply on the aching tooth to alleviate pain

Spasmodic stomach pain: Mix little asafoetida in a glass water and drink. This expels wind from the stomach and also counteracts spasmodic stomach disorders; it also acts as aphrodisiac if used in cooking

Saffron

Saffron or kesar is considered the queen of spices. 70,000 saffron flowers produce only 1 kilogram of saffron. The delicate dried threads of saffron flowers are found in Kashmir. It is the only flower in the world which contains soluble cartone it and is one of the most prestigious spices in the world.

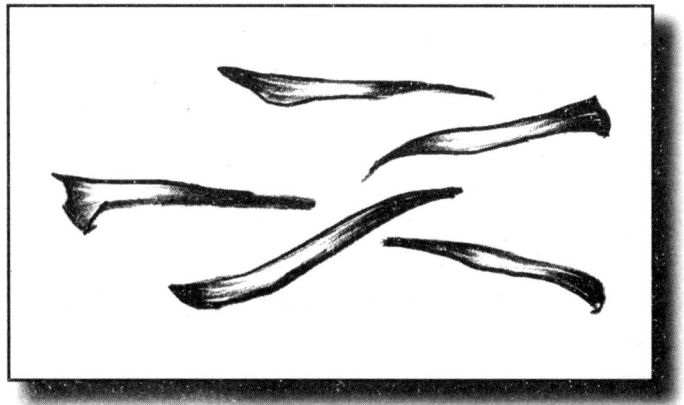

It is anti-cancerous, sedative, antioxidant and a potent aphrodisiac.

It strengthens the heart and the nervous system and reverses the effect of brain degeneration due to alcoholism.

It also helps in the treatment of measles, bladder, kidney and liver disorders.

It also alleviates the side effects of chemotherapy. It cures stomach disorders, flu, cough, cold and asthma and whets appetite.

Aphrodisiac: Saffron is the stigma of the female part of the flower crocus. It has both symbolic and physical aphrodisiacal effect. So, it is a key ingredient for preparing erotic dishes. It makes erogenous zones more sexually alive and responsive.

Inflammation of the gums: Massage a little saffron on the gums to reduce pain and inflammation.

Loss of appetite: Mix saffron in little ginger juice and drink it to cure this condition.

This also cures insomnia as it is a mild sedative.

Fever: Take ¼ teaspoon of saffron, 1 teaspoon of tulsi leaf powder, 2 green cardamoms, 1 teaspoon of cinnamon powder and boil in 2 cups water till it is reduced to 1 cup. Add milk and honey and drink twice a day to reduce fever.

Flu: Take one teaspoon of tulsi leaf powder, ¼ teaspoon cinnamon powder, cardamoms and saffron and boil in 1 cup milk. Add sugar and honey and drink twice a day to be cured of flu.

Saffron regulates menstrual cycle and relieves from nose bleeding, fatigue and exhaustion.

Since this spice produces heat in the body it should be avoided by pregnant ladies as it may bring about abortion. Besides it should not be taken by lactating mothers. Too much of this spice may prove harmful to kidneys and the nervous system. So, it should be used in very small, quantities. To get relief from cold, a paste made of saffron and milk is applied on the forehead and around the nose.

It treats urinary and digestive disorders. If soaked in water for a whole night and mixed with honey and if drunk, it helps free passage of urine. If mixed in 1 teaspoon of ghee and eaten, saffron gives relief in diabetes and also strengthens the heart and the brain. It also regulates menstruation if taken mixed in hot milk. Saffron oil is applied externally to cure uterine sores. It is also helpful in treating liver, kidney and bladder disorders. Saffron fights tumours and alleviates some of the side effects of chemotherapy. It reverses the effects of brain damage due to alcoholism. It is mostly used as colouring and flavouring agent in food

Thymol Seeds

Thymol seeds, (Thymol in Hindi) not only boosts your sex life but it is excellent for curing digestive problems. It is a wonderful cure for acidity and indigestion. Flavonoids in thymol not only prevent flatulence, colds and digestive problems, they cause cancer cells to mutate.

Substitute domain seeds with thymol seeds.

Virility: The seeds should be crushed and fried in pure ghee with an equal quantity of crushed kernels of tamarind seeds and then the mixture should be ground to a paste and preserved in a bottle. A teaspoon of this mixture should be added to a cup of milk with 2 tablespoons of honey and it should be taken before going to bed. This not only increases virility but also cures premature ejaculation.

Indigestion: Mix together half teaspoon of powdered dry ginger and powdered thymol seeds. Eat one teaspoon of this powder with 1 tablespoon of jaggery to get relief.

Acidity: Soak the seeds in lime juice for a few hours and dry it in the sun. Powder it and take a little daily half an hour before meals. It is an excellent remedy for curing acidity.

Cold hands and feet: Apply a paste of thymol seeds on hands and feet to bring back the heat in them.

Scanty menses; Make a tea with thymol seeds and jaggery and drink twice daily to restart the menses.

Stuffed nose: Roast thymol seeds and tie them up in a cloth. Use this for inhaling and fomentation.

Gastro intestinal disorders: Soak thymol in water for a night. Keep the bowl in the open exposed to the light of the moon. Next day, strain out the water, bottle and keep. Use the water in the treatment of diarrhoea, dysentery, dyspepsia and indigestion, this water proves beneficial in the early stages of cholera to check vomiting.

Cholic: 1 teaspoon of thymol seed powder mixed with ½ teaspoon of dry ginger powder and ¼ teaspoon of black salt mixed with 2 tablespoons warm water if taken will give immediate relief.

Flatulence: Thymol seed powder mixed with equal quantities of dry ginger powder and lime juice if taken with warm water helps in curing flatulence.

Common cold: A tablespoon of seeds crushed and tied in a cloth and inhaled or kept near the pillow while sleeping removes nasal congestion.

Rheumatic pain: Thymol seed oil massaged on the painful portions of the body provides relief.

Sore throat: Tea made of these seeds and salt and used as a gargle not only cures sore throat but also hoarseness due to cold.

Influenza: Mix together 1 teaspoon each of tulsi juice and honey and ½ teaspoon each of thymol seed powder and ginger juice. Take twice a day to get relief.

Virility booster: The water of thymol seeds when taken with juice of betel leaves cures digestive disorders. It excels the gripe mixture preparation available in the market.

Cloves

Cloves or (Lavang in Hindi) are obtained from the clove tree (Eugenia aromatics) which grows to a height of 25 to 30 feet. Cloves are the unopened flowers which are plucked carefully and then dried. The word clove is derived from the latin word 'clavus' meaning 'nail' which defines its shape. It is an aromatic stimulant and a warming digestive tonic. The seeds, leaves and stems of cloves have a strong aroma like celery which gives a distinctive aroma and taste to the food.

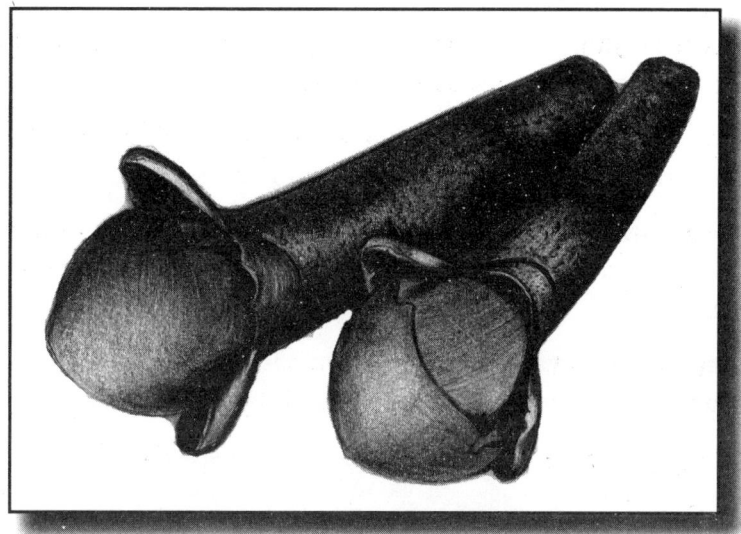

Clove oil has a strong soothing effect and antiseptic properties. It prevents tooth decay and numbs tooth ache. It also combats nausea, digestive and parasite problems in the stomach.

Running nose: Apply a paste of cloves, eucalyptus, camphor and cinnamon on the forehead and nose to stop a running nose.

Vomiting: Clove powder mixed with honey if licked, stops vomiting.

Cholera: Cloves boiled in 2 glasses of water (later reduced to 1 glass) and taken at regular intervals in small doses reduces the severity of the disease.

Cough: Cloves eaten with salt helps in reducing cough.

Tuberculosis: Five drops of clove oil mixed in ¼ teaspoon of garlic juice and 1 teaspoon of honey if taken a few times daily, will reduce the severity of the disease. This also proves helpful in bronchitis.

Asthma: Boil 6 cloves in 1 cup of water till it is reduced to half. Take three times daily with honey.

Ear ache: Boil a clove in sesame seed oil. Cool till bearably hot and put a drop in the aching ear to cure the pain.

Headache: Make a paste of cloves with milk. Add a pinch of salt and apply on the forehead for relief. Salt decreases tension.

Stye in the eye: Rub cloves in rose water to a paste and apply on the stye a few times daily till you get relief

Chronic cough: Chew five roasted cloves with tulsi leaves to get relief.

Pyorrhoea: Grind together tulsi leaves, cloves and camphor to a paste. Make into pea sized pills and keep pressed under the teeth to get relief from this disease and other disorder of the teeth and gums.

Mouth wash: Take ½ cup each of vinegar and white wine, ¼ cup honey and 1 teaspoon ground cloves. Boil for 10 minutes, cool and bottle and use as a mouth wash to clean the mouth and to sweeten the breath and stop foul odour in the mouth.

Chewing whole cloves helps curb the craving of alcohol in alcoholics

Toothache: Apply clove oil on the aching tooth to get relief from toothache.

Stomach ulcers: ½ teaspoon powder of cloves mixed in cold milk and taken once everyday helps in stomach ulcers. This also helps in stimulating the digestive system and prevents damage to the cells.

Black Pepper

Black pepper grows on a large (woody vine) which grows to the height of 30 feet. The vine bears white flowers after a long wait of four years. These white flowers develop into berries which are known as peppercorns. Pepper is a priced spice since ancient times. In ancient Greece peppercorns were used as a currency and as an offering to Gods. In the Middle Ages, wealth of a person was measured by the stock of peppercorns he possessed because of its medicinal properties. It was cherished by everyone. In Europe, pepper was considered so valuable that when Alarcita Goth conquered Rome in 400 A.D, he demanded 3000 pounds of peppercorns as part of the city's ransom.

Besides being of high medicinal value it is used for its pungency to spice up food and it is also a very good preservative. So, it is used widely in foods.

It not only fights disease but also maintains the body bestowing good health. It also promotes sweating thereby helping in removing toxins from the body and is also diuretic (promotes urination).

Spices

Pepper reduces flatulence, induces sweating, prevents water retention, stimulates the taste buds increases the production of stomach acids and improves digestion.

It also has snit-bacterial and anti-oxidant properties and helps in breaking down fat cells.

Constipation: Few slices of raw papaya seasoned with pepper and cumin seeds powder and black salt cures indigestion and constipation.

Cold cough: Take 1 tablespoon sugar, 8 tulsi leaves, 4 peppercorns and equal amount of elendil pili powder and ¼ teaspoon of asthamudi powder and boil in 1 cup water for 5 minutes. Strain and drink as hot as possible at bedtime to cure cough and cold.

Digestive problems: Pepper improves the digestion because it stimulates the taste buds thereby making the stomach secrete hydrochloric acid which aids in the digestion of food. Insufficient production of this acid leads to heartburn and acidity.

Obesity: The outer layer of the peppercorns breaks down fat cells and keeps you slim and trim.

Dry cough: Chewing a few peppercorns and keeping a few in the mouth helps in curing dry cough and irritation of the throat. Sprinkling pepper powder on hot tea and drinking bit helps in curing persistent cough.

Hoarseness: Boil jaggery, peppercorns in water with a pinch of salt. Strain and drink it piping hot to be cured.

Heat in the body: Eat 6 peppercorns with 10 tulsi leaves. This also relieves pain in the heart.

Ear ache: Boil tulsi leaves and peppercorns in mustard oil till they turn black. Strain and bottle it. Use it in aching ear after warming it to get relief. This mixture also cures deafness.

Toothache: This is cured by massaging the teeth with a paste made of 10 tulsi leaves and six peppercorns.

Typhoid: Make a paste of 2 teaspoons of tulsi leaves, 1 teaspoon pepper powder and half teaspoon honey. Take this mixture 2 to 3 times per day to get relief.

Diabetes: Take 10 of each–peppercorns, bilwa (a fruit found in the sub-Himalayan forest), neem, holy basil (tulsi) and curry leaves and boil in 1 glass of water till it is reduced to one-fourth its original quantity. Take this first thing in the morning to reduce blood sugar levels in the body.

Always be careful when using spices because excess will harm your body. Same is the case with peppercorns; if used in excess they may lead to gastric bleeding and other bleeding in the body.

Fennel

Fennel (Sauf in Hindi) is a product of the apiaceae family. It is used in cooking and also in medicines. It forms a base for many cough mixtures and medicinal lozenges.

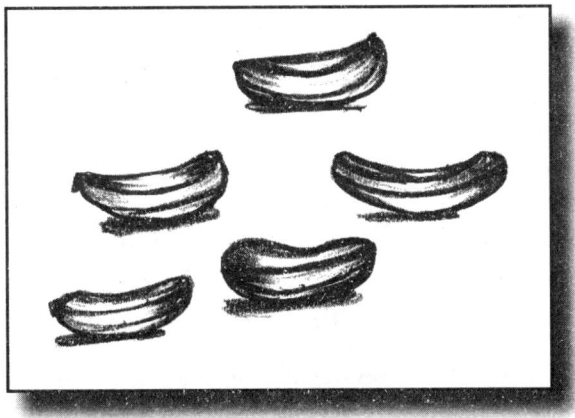

Digestive disorders: Boil 1 tablespoon of fennel seeds in 1 cup water till it is reduced to half. Drink it after sweetening with sugar. This is beneficial in the treatment of indigestion, flatulence, dyspepsia and other digestive disorders.

Colic: Fennel seeds help to relieve colic in babies. Powdered and combined with equal quantities of powdered black cumin seeds and powdered peppermint tablets, this powder if given in tiny doses to the babies will help relieve their colic.

Menstrual disorders: Boil 1 tablespoon of fennel seeds in one cup of water till it is reduced to half. This mixture when sweetened with sugar and taken internally relieves painful menstruation and regularizes periods. This mixture is also helpful for jaundice patients.

Sore or inflamed eyes: Soak fennel seeds in distilled water for a whole night. Next morning strain and bottle. Use this water for cleaning the eyes. This water gives great relief in eye problems.

Digestive problems: Take 1 tablespoon fennel seeds, 20 black grapes and 1/8th teaspoon asafetida. Boil in 1 cup of water and puree the mixture in the blender. Taken internally it cures almost all the digestive problems.

Insomnia: Dissolve ½ teaspoon of cumin seed powder and 1 teaspoon fennel seed powder in 1 cup milk. Sweeten with honey and drink before going to bed. This will cure insomnia. It will provides health to the brain. You can massage the forehead with fennel seed powder mixed to a paste in pure ghee this will also cure you of insomnia.

Aphrodisiac: These seeds are said to have the power of increasing sexual desire. Chewing on these seeds with honey regularly is an excellent way to increase your sexuality.

Scanty menses: Drinking tea made with fennel seeds for 1 week at a stretch will regularise the menstrual cycle.

Indigestion: Take a teaspoon of fennel seed powder, half teaspoon of cardamom seed powder and mix in 1 cup of hot water along with a tablespoon honey. Drink three times daily to get relief.

Turmeric

Amongst all the spices, turmeric is a virtual gold mine. Not only does it fight the diseases of the heart, but it also reduces the risk of cancer and is anti-inflammatory. Turmeric was cultivated in Harappa as early as 3000 B.C It tastes pungent, bitter and is slightly sweet. It has a deep yellow colour and is a preservative of the highest kind. So it is used in pickles for preserving them and also in food to give it colour, taste and aroma. It is also associated with Indian rituals also.

Turmeric contains an anti-oxidant phytochemical which not only acts as a preservative to food items but also protects the body against a variety of diseases. It improves liver functioning and digestion and also reduces inflammation in the body. It heals wounds, cuts and injuries both external and internal.

It also helps in the treatment of arthritis and other joint pains, combats skin allergies and respiratory diseases as well. It is also known as the blood purifier and beautifier of the skin. That is why a number of cosmetics have turmeric as one of their main ingredients. It helps neutralise free radicals, the cell damaging molecules in the body. If unabated these free radicals can cause diseases like cancer arthritis and heart disease.

It is also known to inhibit excessive blood clotting which is the leading cause of disease of the heart and joint pain. It also delays the onset of Alzheimer disease.

Cancer: Curcumin a flavonoid within turmeric is antioxidant responsible for anti-cancer, anti-inflammatory effects in the body.

Blood purification: Turmeric is a great purifier of blood. It also stimulates the liver, increases red blood cell formation, inhibits the red blood cell clumping and increases blood circulation.

Skin: Since turmeric purifies the blood, it gives a skin a glowing look. The skin becomes soft and smooth and free of embarrassing blemishes. Here is beautifying oil for the skin. Mix 50 grams of turmeric powder in ½ litre of sesame seed oil. Set in the sun and then in the light of the moon for 15 days. Strain and use it on the skin to make it for a wonderfully beautiful.

Canker sores: Mix turmeric with honey and apply on the sores to get relief.

Pimples: Mix together coriander and mint leaf juice with a pinch of turmeric and camphor powder and apply regularly on the pimples to get rid of them.

Diabetes: Equal quantities of dried amla powder, jamun seed powder and turmeric powder if taken morning and evening with water, will bring down sugar levels.

Cold: Take a glass of hot milk in which ½ teaspoon of turmeric powder has been mixed.

Wounds: Make a paste of turmeric powder and apply on the wounds to protect the body from infection and a speedy recovery. Application of turmeric powder on the wounds prevent the formation of pus. If the pus is already formed, wash your hands with a good antiseptic soap, press the sides of the wound to remove pus. Fill the wound with turmeric powder. After some time, some fluid will come out. Clean it and fill the wound with fresh turmeric powder. Repeat this till the fluid stops and the wound is cured.

Arthritis: Boil 5 grams of turmeric powder in 200 ml of cows milk and water. Simmer it for 5 minutes and then add a teaspoon of sugar. Drink this to cure arthritis and infection of the upper respiratory tract.

Eczema: Apply turmeric juice squeezed out from fresh turmeric on the ringworm. Also consume ¼ teaspoon of turmeric powder with 1 tablespoon of honey in empty stomach.

Pain and inflammation: Apply warm sesame seed oil on the affected parts and after 2 hours, gently rub turmeric powder over the oil. Keep on rubbing till the oil is absorbed. Repeat this for 2 weeks to relieve the pain and inflammation.

Besides the above diseases, turmeric is heart healthy. Since it lowers cholesterol, it prevents heart attacks. As it is a rich source of antioxidants, it prevents liver disorders. Besides, it is anti inflammatory and anti-cancer as well.

Blood cancer: Turmeric powder is said to ward of cancer of the blood. According to the recent research conducted by Dr M, Ngabhushan and V. Ramaswamy it is found that turmeric contains antioxidant properties which gives protection against environmental chemicals that damage DNA. Turmeric contains curcumins which exhibit anti-bacterial and anti-fungal activity which helps in warding off leukemia. Today this spice is known as yellow gold all over the world.

Turmeric protects the liver from toxic compounds, improves the circulation of blood and fights atherosclerosis.

Boils: Roast turmeric powder, dissolve in water and apply on boils. This solution helps the boils to burst. Likewise you can apply the paste of black cumin seeds mixed with turmeric powder on the boils to get relief. Bitter gourd juice mixed with lime juice and a pinch of turmeric powder if taken in empty stomach also cures boils.

Turmeric is carminative and antiseptic and used in the cure of diabetes and leprosy.

In chicken pox and small pox it is made into a paste with neem leaves and oil and applied on the body. Juice of the fresh root of turmeric if taken internally and applied externally, helps in curing and warding numerous skin infections and ailments.

Paste of turmeric mixed with water if applied before taking a bath clears the skin of all its blemishes including pimples. Turmeric removes gas formation in the body. It lowers the risk of breast, lung, prostrate and colon cancers. It also alleviates leukemia and helps in Alzheimer's disease. It also gives relief in the internal haemorrhage, menstrual difficulties and blood in the urine.

Cinnamon

In ancient times cinnamon was considered more precious than gold because of its varied properties of healing. It is obtained from the bark of a tree belonging to the laurel family. It is chiefly grown in Ceylon and some parts of India. It has a pleasant taste, aroma and flavour and so it is used extensively in food. Cinnamon sticks are often used in hot drinks such as mulled wine, hot chocolate and coffee to add that extra zing to a cold night.

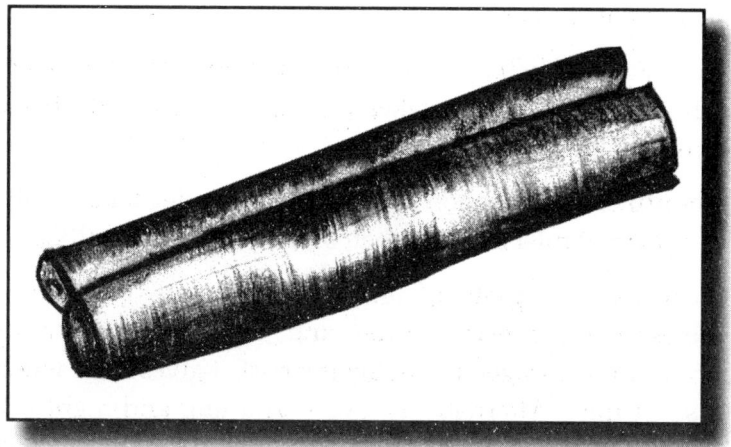

It has many uses besides being a condiment. When buying cinnamon choose those which has a light colour, are wafer thin and rolled into long sticks.

This spice is a sedative, reduces the severity of fits in epilepsy, an antibiotic, diuretic and anti-ulcer.

Diabetes: It controls blood sugar by regulating insulin levels in the body. 1 teaspoon of cinnamon powder should be taken in 1 glass of orange juice to get relief.

Heart disease: It contains antioxidants which reduce cholesterol levels in the body and revitalizes the arteries and the veins in the heart. It also increases the circulation of the blood and is a blood thinning agent.

Irritable bowel syndrome-Small amounts cinnamon if taken regularly helps in this condition and other stomach ailments. Since it is a rich source of iron, calcium and dietary fibre, it helps to improve the health of the colon.

Menstrual cramps: If taken in small amounts in a cup of milk sweetened with honey, it proves effective in controlling menstrual cramps.

Common cold: Tea made with cinnamon powder, honey, ginger and lime juice if taken piping hot, proves effective in curing cold.

Vomiting: 1/4 teaspoon of cinnamon powder taken with 1 teaspoon of tulsi leaf juice helps in controlling vomiting.

Arthritis: If a paste of one tablespoon full of honey, 2 tablespoons of warm water and 1 teaspoon cinnamon powder is massaged on the aching part, it gives relief within a short time. Alternatively, every morning and night take 1 cup hot of water with 2 teaspoons of honey mixed with 1 teaspoon of cinnamon powder. If is taken regularly, this mixture it can even cure chronic arthritis.

Cinnamon improves cholesterol metabolism and so it is highly effective for patients who suffer from high cholesterol problem.

Cinnamon oil is a powerful stimulant and is used for gastric problems, flatulence, cholic and rheumatism. Cinnamon has fragrant and a pleasant flavour and so it is used in a variety of foods. The powder of this spice can be sprinkled on tea, coffee and a variety of desserts for a unique and a delightful flavour. Cinnamon is a hot and warm spice so it should be consumed with caution.

Hair loss: Take 2 tablespoons of hot olive oil and mix with 1 teaspoon of cinnamon powder. Massage in the head, keep for 15 minutes and then wash with a mild soap or shampoo. This not only cures hair loss but it cures even baldness.

Gas: 1 teaspoon of honey if mixed with half teaspoon of cinnamon powder if taken daily can relieve gas. Cinnamon powder if taken before meals relieves acidity and digests even the heaviest of meals. It is also effective in fighting vaginal yeast infections, oral yeast infections and stomach ulcers. It also boosts brain power, you should exercise caution when eating cinnamon because in large doses it can be toxic to the body.

Mustard Seeds

Mustard seeds are obtained from the mustard plant. It is related to broccoli and cabbage. There are forty different varieties of mustard plants but there are three principal varieties which are in use. These are black mustard seeds, yellow mustard seeds and brown mustard seeds.

Black mustard seeds have the most pungent taste and aroma; yellow mustard seeds are mild in taste and aroma and brown mustard seeds have a pungent acid taste and it is used to make Dijon mustard which is used in mayonnaise sauce and other food items.

Mustard seeds are an ancient spice whose mention was made 5000 years ago. It is also mentioned in the New Testament in which the kingdom of heaven is compared to a grain of mustard.

Mustard seeds have been used since ancient times for medicinal and culinary purposes. Hippocrates, the father of modern medicine advised people to use mustard for external and internal usage. Pythagoras, the Greek philosopher wrote about this seed and its uses in medicine.

This seed has the unique honour of being written about in the holy bible.

Asthma: As this seed is rich in selenium, a nutrient which helps in reducing the severity of asthma, asthma patients should use this seed regularly in food. It also helps prevent cancer and rheumatoid arthritis.

Blood pressure: Since these seeds are rich in magnesium, it has the ability of lowering high blood pressure.

Migraine: Daily intake of these wonder seeds lessens the severity of menopause systems, helps in migraine attacks and diabetes and heart problems.

Cancer: Soak 1 teaspoon of seeds in water for a few hours and then consume them to cut down the risk of gastro-intestinal cancers.

Since these seeds are rich in omega-3 fatty acids, they are very heart friendly. As these seeds contain goitrogens a natural substance found in them, it can interfere with the functioning of the thyroid gland. So people suffering from thyroid problems should avoid them.

CHAPTER 3

Pulses and Lentils

Pulses and lentils were amongst the first foods cultivated by man. They are not only rich in proteins but also in essential amino acids. If we combine pulses and grains as in khichadi, idli or dosa etc then we get more proteins in the body.

Thus, we find high quality proteins in the combination of lentils, pulses and rice or lentils and wheat and other grains.

The nourishing value of pulses and lentils was seem form early biblical times. The first chapter of the 'Book of Daniel' says how Daniel was taken captive into Babylon and he refused to defile himself with the kings offerings of meat and wine. He asked the servants to serve him and his three companions with pulses and water instead at the end of ten days. Daniel and his companions looked healthier than before than the young men who ate meat and wine.

In addition to their high protein they are also an excellent sources of B vitamins especially Vitamin B6 and folacin. Dried beans however are deficient in Vitamin A and C which need to be supplied by vegetables and fruits. So, whenever you eat pulses and lentils they should be accompanied by vegetables and fruits.

Whenever you buy lentils you should also buy pulses and the combination of the two should be the mainstay of your meals. This combination supplies more nutrition to the body like chickpeas (Kabuli chana in Hindi) cooked with split Bengal gram (Chana dal or rajmah in Hindi) cooked with black lentil (Masoor dal in Hindi) etc.

Use of fermented lentils, pulses and grains increases the nutritional value of these foods by almost six times. Buy unpolished and unrefined grains and cereals. These are more nutritious then the polished grains.

Soya Beans

Soya bean is the world's most useful and cheapest source of proteins. It is said to be one of the best health foods and is a store house of nutrients. It is a staple food in many Asian countries and amongst the vegetarians all over the world. It comes from an annual plant and is a member of the same family as peas. It contains forty percent proteins as compared to the eighteen percent found in beef and fish. The beans are a store house of vitamins A, C, K and B. Besides, it contains minerals like potassium, iron, phosphorus and calcium, the bean is low in saturated fat and provides an easily assimilable form of essential amino acids our body requires making it a complete protein.

Soya beans can benefit anyone right from a baby to the menopausal woman, to the man suffering from heart disease, diabetes or cancer. The low incidence of colon and breast cancer in China and Japan has been partially attributed to the high consumption of soya beans.

The low incidence of menopausal symptoms in Japanese women has been attributed to consumption of soya based products.

Soya diets have also been shown to lower bad cholesterol. It contains many individual isoflavones but the most beneficial are genistein and daidzein. The highest amounts of isoflavones and soya proteins are found in soya nuts, tofu, soya milk and soya flour.

Soya proteins and isoflavones lower LDL the bad cholesterol in the body and decreases blood clotting which reduces the risk of heart attacks and strokes.

They also provide antioxidants which reduces artery clogging plaque, stabilizes blood pressure and promotes healthy blood vessels. This protects the body from radical damage, boosts the immune system and lowers the risk of atherosclerosis heart, disease and hypertension.

Soya bean soluble fibre protects the body from many digestive related diseases such as cancers of the colon, urine and prostrate.

Soya proteins enhances the body's ability to retain and better absorb the calcium in the bones whilst its inflavones slow bone loss and inhibit bone break down which help prevents osteoporosis and even reverses its effects. They also help the body regulate estrogen levels which help remove many menopausal symptoms. It has been noticed that isoflavonas function similarly to HRT without producing the risk associated with this controversial treatment. It also relieves hot flushes, night sweats, fatigue and vaginal dryness which are all associated with menopause.

Soya proteins and soluble fibre it contains help regulate glucose; levels in the body and helps in regulating kidney filtration which helps control diabetes and kidney disease.

Tofu, a food made from soya bean curd is a popular culinary item in eastern Asia and its neighbouring regions. The ancient Chinese considered soya beans as their most important crop and one of the five sacred grains required for a healthy life.

Firm tofu fried, stir fried, deep fried, sauted and made into dishes with other vegetables or added to salads eat all to good health. Silken tofu on the other hand is used for dips and spreads, sauces and sweet dishes. Besides having a high protein content, tofu also contains Vitamins B1, B2 and B3.

Tofu is a good source of soya protein. Regular use of tofu in diet lowers cholesterol, triglyceride levels, reduces the tendency of platelets which form clots in the blood and also raises the levels of good cholesterol. Tofu is helpful in alleviating the symptoms of menopause. It contains phytoestrogens which helps the fluctuation of estrogen in menopausal women and helps her maintain her inner balance.

Tofu helps in strengthening bones and teeth and improves the nervous system and also cures anaemia because it is a rich source of iron and calcium.

Soya milk is a very good alternative to cow and buffalo milk. Compared to these milk, soya milk has a lower fat content, lower proportion of saturated fat and no cholesterol. It is low in carbohydrates and is a good source of proteins. Soya bean curd has many medicinal properties. It is alkaline in nature which improves complexion, stimulates both growth of the body and removes constipation.

Soya bean flour can be used in a variety of products like sweets, chapaties, cakes, biscuits etc. It is also used in baby food and other low calorie foods. Soya grits are used in sweets and in processed meats as pies and sausages. Both soya flour and grits go into baked goods and pet foods and into 'textured vegetable proteins' or TVP foods. These foods are chemically treated to look and taste like meat so that they appeal to consumers who are diehard non-vegetarians. TVP foods can be mixed with meat or eaten alone. They cost less than meat and contain more protein than meat. Soya bean granules and chunks are the most popular ingredients to be used in TVP foods.

Soya bean oil is another product of this miracle golden bean. It is rich in proteins, carbohydrates, vitamins and minerals. It is an oil which should be used by all health conscious individuals.

Soya sauce is one of the world's oldest condiments. It is prepared from pickled soya beans. It was discovered nearly 2500 years ago in China and since then it has remained a major ingredient in many Asian cuisines. It is believed that in the 6th century B.C when Buddhism became very popular in Japan and China, vegetarianism created a need for meatless dishes. Japanese priests while studying in China discovered this sauce by using fermented a paste of salty soya beans. Soya bean sauce has a remarkable aroma which adds a unique flavour and richness to all the foods it touches.

Soya beans provide more proteins than most of the other vegetables, grains, pulses and lentils.

Diabetes: Soya bean products are excellent food for diabetics. Their carbohydrates provide energy in the body without causing sugar to appear in the urine.

Kidney and urinary infections: Soya bean milk if taken regularly is excellent for curing kidney and bladder infections.

Anaemia-Soya beans are rich in iron. If taken regularly they cure anaemia.

Nervous disorders: Soya milk mixed with honey if taken before sleeping in the night is invaluable for curing nervous disorders, insomnia, forgetfulness and hysteria.

Underweight babies: If under weight babies are given soya bean milk instead of ordinary milk it increases their weight.

Dandruff: Mix soya bean powder with water and massage on the scalp. Wash off after half an hour with a mild shampoo. This removes dandruff completely. Certain nutrients in soya beans like biotin, lecithin zinc and selenium not only prevent dandruff but also cures it.

Constipation: Regular intake of soya beans removes constipation, improves the complexion and helps in curing retarded growth.

Skin disorders: If soya beans are eaten regularly, they improve the health of the skin and is especially beneficial in curing itching and skin lesions.

Dull and yellow skin: Soya bean powder mixed with curds and applied on the skin for half an hour every week, removes dullness and imparts a healthy glow to the skin.

Bengal Gram

Bengal gram is full of medicinal properties. It contains proteins, fibre, carbohydrates, cretonne and Vitamins B and C. Sprouted Bengal gram contains fifty percent more of Vitamin B and C and so a soup prepared from it makes an ideal food for children and sick people. If soaked whole night in water and eaten in the morning with honey, it nourishes and strengthens the body.

Diabetes: Drinking water in which this lentil has been boiled enhances the utilization of glucose in the body and shows considerable improvement in the blood sugar a level and also stops the appearance of sugar in the urine.

Anaemia: 1 tablespoon of juice of leaves of Bengal gram tree taken with 1 teaspoon of honey daily cures anaemia since its leaves are chock full of iron.

Pimples: 1 tablespoon flour of Bengal grams mixed with 1 teaspoon each of coriander and mint leaf juice to a paste and applied on the pimply face is a sure cure for pimples. This paste also cures eczema and scabies.

Cleansing agent: Bengal gram flour when mixed with juice of neem leaves and if applied on allergic skin, eczema, scabies and other skin diseases and left for 20 minutes and washed with rose water not only makes a good cleansing agent for the skin but also helps in curing these diseases.

Impotence: 2 tablespoon of flour of puffed gram dal (roasted chana in Hindi) mixed with 1 teaspoon each of sugar, milk powder and ground dates is a sure remedy in curing this disease.

Excesses menses: Fry 2 tablespoons of powdered puffed gram dal (chana) in 4 tablespoons of pure ghee to a golden colour. Add half a cup of milk. Cook till dry. Mix in 2 tablespoons each of sliced almonds and pistachios and eat from the first day of menses to fourth day in empty stomach to get relief.

Rough skin: Mix 2 tablespoons of Bengal gram flour with 1 tablespoon of orange peel powder and 2 tablespoons of cream. Apply on the skin and leave for 20 minutes and then wash off. This gives a smooth and soft skin.

Cold: This lentil is an excellent remedy for common cold. Make a soup of 2 tablespoons of this lentil with 1 big tomato. Spice in with red chilli powder and sip it piping hot to be cured of cold.

Obesity: Since this lentil is rich in fibre and zinc, it causes in rise the leptin levels. This hormone plays a role in making you feel satiated. So, do not overeat. With lentin in the body there is very less chance of fat being stored in the body.

 ## Green Gram

Green gram or (Mung dal in Hindi) is a very wholesome food. It is free from heaviness and therefore it does not encourage the formation of gas like other lentils. So, even children, babies, sick and invalids can take it. This dal comes in three varieties, the yellow variety, the whole green dried seed which is mostly sprouted and used in salads and dishes and split green dal in which the seed is split in two parts. This dal is mostly used for making khichadi in combination with rice.

Yellow mung dal is highly nutritious food for babies invalids, sick and old people.

Since it is rich in iron, carotene, B vitamins, calcium, phosphorus and carbohydrates, its regular use during pregnancy and lactation gives health to the mother.

Its soup made with dal, tomatoes, coriander curry leaves and ginger is the best article of diet when recovering from any illness. The sprouted whole mung dal is much more nutritious than the other mung dals. So try to consume sprouted mung as much as possible.

Fever: A cup of water in which the lentil has been boiled is excellent for combating the ill effects of diseases like cholera, typhoid, chickenpox, jaundice and appendicitis.

Arthritis: Soup of this lentil prepared with garlic and spiced with fenugreek seed powder if taken daily relieves pain in the joints.

Burning eyes: Powdered mung dal mixed with rice water to a paste and applied over the eyelids of the affected eyes removes burning from the eyes.

Dark skin: Powder this dal and mix this with buttermilk with a pinch of turmeric powder. If this mixture is applied on the skin and removed after 20 minutes with water, it helps in whitening and brightening the skin. It is an excellent detergent for using instead of soap, especially it makes a good cleanser for sensitive skin. If this paste is used for shampooing the hair, the hair turns healthy and the growth of hair thickens and it also cures the hair of dandruff.

Heavy menses: Take two tablespoons of flour of whole mung dal. Fry in 4 tablespoons of ghee to a golden colour. Add 1 cup ghee to 2 tablespoons of sugar and cook till dry. Mix in 1 tablespoon each of sliced dates, raisins and almonds and pistachios. Eat from the first day of the menstrual cycle to the fourth day to get relief.

CHAPTER 4

Grains

Grains belong to the plant family and amongst the most famous grains in the world are rice and wheat. Grains also include bajra, jowar, rajgira and barley. They are very rich sources of fibre and help to lower cholesterol.

But you should opt for organically grown grains. Ordinary grains are full of chemicals, preservatives and addictives which cause disease in the body because they are high in free radicals which give rise to heart disease cancer, osteoporosis and other dangerous diseases.

Wheat which is unhusked is very essential for maintaining the health of the body. The bran is the outer husk of the wheat and wheat germ is the kernel of the wheat. Wheat is chock full of fibre. Therefore, it reduces one risk of colon and rectal cancers.

Wheat is also an excellent source of B vitamins, iron, phosphorus and trace of other vitamins. The germ is rich in proteins and oils. The germ contains 6 to 8 times as much riboflavin as the whole wheat, plus thiamine, Vitamin E and traces of minerals such as zinc, copper, magnesium and iron.

Some people are allergic to wheat; they can eat bajra flour. Since wheat is rich in carbohydrates people suffering from high diabetes should avoid wheat and subsist on bajra flour.

Like wheat, rice too is the mainstay of every meal. Without rice and wheat the stomach will be satiated. But one should eat unpolished and brown rice because this has more nutrients than polished rice.

Wheat

Out of the 300 families of flowering plants, the greatest importance to mankind is the grass family to which our grains like wheat, rice, oats, rye, barley and millets belong. Grains have remained the chief articles of diet to all mankind but the most popular grains throughout the world are rice and wheat. Bread, chapaties, biscuits, cakes etc are all made of wheat and they have remained throughout the centuries our chief articles of diet which is not only economical but also very essential source of energy to the body. Its nutritive value varies with the part of the grain used. Refined flour furnishes mostly starch and proteins with very little more unless enriched with iron and B vitamins which are lost in the milling process.

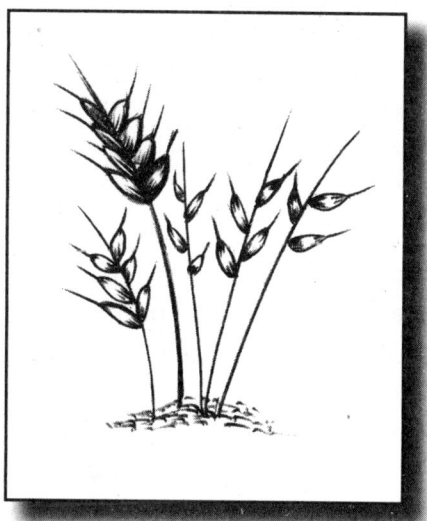

On the other hand, whole grain wheat is excellent source of B vitamins, phosphorus, iron and traces of other minerals. It provides more than 2 dozen nutrients.

The outer layer of the kernel provides not only most of the minerals but the cellulose or fibre which provides bulk to the body and regulates the absorption and excretion of nutrients from the elementary tract.

The germ is rich in proteins and oils. It contains 6 to 8 times as much riboflavin as the whole wheat plus thiamine, Vitamin E and traces of minerals such as zinc, copper, iron and magnesium.

Due to its excellent nutritive value wheat should be eaten regularly. One or two servings should be eaten at every meal in the form of chapaties, whole grain bread, cooked wheat as in dalia or pasta products such as macaroni, spaghetti or noodles.

According to a study conducted by Harvard medical school, women who ate whole grains were 49 percent less likely to gain weight compared to those eating foods made out of refined flour and other refined grains. Wheat bran is said to decrease the metabolism of estrogen that is known to reduce the incidence of breast cancer in premenstrual women between the ages of 45 to 55

Women who ate 3 to 4 high fibre muffins or chapaties per day made of wheat bran decreased their blood estrogen levels by seventeen percent in 2 months by accelerating the metabolism of estrogen and occupying estrogen receptors in the body. Components of whole wheat appear to have a dual function which decreases the chances of breast cancer. Wheat bran also prevents cancer by promoting changes in the colon. It is known as cancer fighter, if taken daily. 28 grams of bran internally will prevent colon polyps (precancerous tumours). So it is wise to include wheat bran and wheat fibre in any form in your daily diet.

Grains

Deep cleanser: Mix together wheat flour with milk cream (found on top of boiled and cooled milk) to a paste. Apply this paste on the face and keep on massaging the face till all the paste falls off and then wash off the paste with water. This paste not only cleanses the skin but also removes dead cells and puts a glow in the skin.

Open pores: Mix half teaspoon of wheat flour with tomato juice to a paste. Apply on the face for 20 minutes and then wash off with plain water.

Dry skin: Mix 1 tablespoon of wheat flour, 1 teaspoon of oil with enough full cream milk. Massage this paste on the face. Wash off with water after 15 minutes.

Oily skin: Mix 1 tablespoon wheat flour with ½ teaspoon lime juice, a pinch of turmeric. Add enough curd to form a paste. Massage into the face and wash off with plain water after 15 minutes.

Pus boils: Roast 2 tablespoons wheat flour lightly. Mix in 1 teaspoon powdered flax seeds. Apply on the pus boils while bearably hot. Tie a bandage over this and remove after 24 hours. The boil will burst till then. Clean up the boil with hydrogen peroxide solution and dust boric acid powder on this. Do not bandage. Let the boil dry up in open air. Within a few days the boil will heal.

Rice

Rice is the staple food of more then half the world's population. Starch constitutes the bulk of the rice grain besides it also contains proteins.

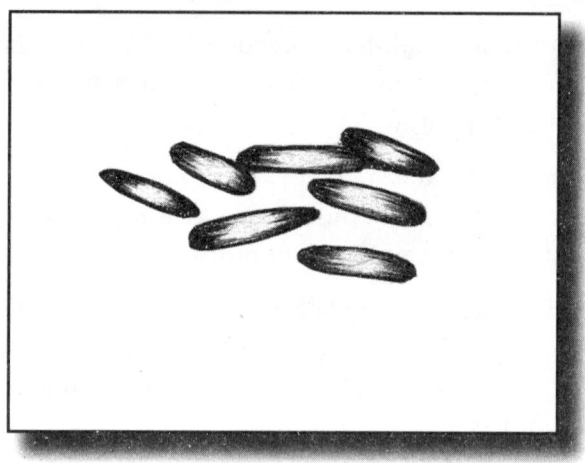

Brown rice is better than polished rice since in the process of processing the rice, it loses some of its minerals and B vitamins present in it.

Brown rice has been shown to contain elements needed for maintaining good and sound health; because of its excellent nutritive value one should try to eat brown rice rather than white rice. One or two servings should be consumed at every meal.

The best way to prepare brown rice is to cook 1 cup brown rice in 2 and half cups of salted water or vegetable broth. Cover and simmer on a slow fire till almost cooked. Just before serving toss it lightly with ½ cup toasted pumpkin seeds, ground nuts or other chopped nuts of your choice. This dish is not only delicious in taste, but the combination of rice with seeds and nuts makes it a very high quality protein dish.

Internal rejuvenation: Rice proteins which comprises upto eight percent of the grain and also contains amino acids in a delicately balanced proportion. A complete internal rejuvenation takes place when rice protein is metabolized into health building amino acids. These amino acids build healthy muscles, skin and hair and maintains a clear eye sight. They nourish the heart, lungs, tendons, ligaments, brain, nervous and glandular systems.

Brown rice besides containing the essential amino acids is also a rich source of B vitamins and so this rice also nourishes the skin, blood vessels and hormonal system, heals wounds and regulates the blood pressure. It also has iron which enriches the blood stream and potassium and phosphorus to maintain the internal water balance of the body.

Hypertension: Rice is low in fat and cholesterol. It has been noted by scientists that where ever rice is used as the main item of food there is very low rate of high blood pressure. Calcium found in brown rice soothes and relaxes the nervous system and helps remove the symptoms of high blood pressure.

Disorders of the digestive system: Rice khichadi mixed with one glass milk and a ripe banana eaten twice daily is a highly nutritional supplement for patients of typhoid, gastric ulcers, cancer of the intestines, colitis, diarrhoea, dysentery, piles, rectal fissures, indigestion, hepatitis, jaundice, morning sickness, acute dilation of the stomach burning and indigestion due to hernia and exclusive accumulation of wind in the stomach

Skin inflammation: Rice flour dusted thickly over the surfaces of diseases like smallpox, measles, prickly heat and other inflammatory infections of the skin helps to cure these conditions.

Burns and scalds: Rice flour spread thickly on burns and scalds removes heat and irritation in the cases of burns and scalds when used immediately after the injury.

Skin food: Mix 2 tablespoons soft cooked rice with 1 egg yolk 1 teaspoon oil and honey and 5 drops of lime juice. Apply on the skin for 15 minutes and then wash off. This pack clears the skin and softens and brightens it.

Smooth skin: Mix 2 tablespoons of kanji or water in which the rice was boiled with 1 tablespoon milk and apply on the skin for half an hour to get a smooth skin.

Leucorrhea: Take daily 2 tablespoons of tulsi juice mixed in 1 cup kanji and restrict the diet to rice and milk for some days till you are cured of your ailment.

Diabetics are not allowed to eat rice, but if you remove the starch from the rice you can enjoy rice. Boil 1 cup rice in 3 cups water till the rice is cooked. Drain out the water completely and then use it.

Barley

Barley resembles wheat but although it is not a very popular grain, it is much healthier than wheat. It is an excellent body builder, after its outer husk is removed and it is then sold as pearl barley. This grain is a very rich source of proteins and B vitamins.

Diarrhoea: Put ¼ cup barley in 2 cups water. When the water is reduced to 1 cup, strain and add juice of 1 lime and sweeten with honey and drink in sips. It not only cures disorders of the digestive system but also cures diarrhoea and ulcers and rejuvenates the body.

Barley brew is a rich source of phosphorus. So it helps in nervous disorders and neuritis. This brew also helps in gaining weight because besides phosphorus it also contains iron. It also helps overcome weakness in the body due to any type of fever.

Urinary disorders: Put ¼ cup barley in 2 cups water. When the water is reduced to 1 cup, strain and mix in a glass of buttermilk. This is highly beneficial in curing burning in the urine, cystitis and nephritis.

Health drink: Put ¼ cup barley to cook in 2 cups of water. When it is reduced to 1 cup, mix in 1 glass milk, 25 grams of raisins and 4 tablespoons of jaggery. Blend in the blender till smooth. This makes a complete health drink.

CHAPTER 5

Nuts

Nuts contain carbohydrates, vitamins and a wide range of minerals. Nuts are a highly concentrated source of food. Most of their stored energy comes in the form of fat but they are also rich in high quality proteins. So, they make a good substitute for meat. The vegetarians who eat meatless diet should include nuts in their diet to get proteins. Due to their high fat content nuts should be used in moderate quantity only. When ground to a powder, nuts are more easily digested than whole nuts.

The fat in nuts is more unsaturated than animal fats and therefore preferable to the latter. They supply essential minerals such as iron, phosphorus, zinc, calcium and B vitamins.

Nuts become easily rancid because of their high fat content. So they should be stored in the fridge in an airtight container. Unshelled nuts stay for longer periods than the shelled ones. Nuts like almonds, walnuts and raisins contain healthy fats which do not clog the arteries.

They are also good sources of proteins, dietary fibre and important minerals like magnesium and copper which help in lipid metabolism and formation of blood.

Nuts are heart friendly; they lower bad cholesterol levels in the blood they also contain omega-3 fatty acids and arginine an amino a acid which increases the production of nitric acid in the body which prevents blood clotting in the arteries.

Nuts have unsaturated fats but since they are high in calories you should not binge on them. They should be eaten in small quantities like 3 walnuts or 6 almonds, 10 pistachios or 30 ground nuts at a time per day

Almond

The almond tree is called phylls by the Greeks because of the legend of the Threcian queen who died of grief because her husband did not return from the Trojan War. The Gods were so moved by her grief that they turned her into an almond tree. All over the world this nut is considered as a symbol of fortune, happiness and health. It was the Moghuls who popularized this nut in India by adding to their cuisine and enhancing the taste and flavour of this dish they touched.

There are two kinds of almonds the bitter and the sweet. Bitter almonds contain traces of prussic acids which causes harm to the body, but of the acid is removed and almond oil is produced, it can be safely used.

After the extraction of almond oil, almond essence is obtained by fermentation and distillation. They are high in proteins, fats, Vitamin E, phosphorous, magnesium and calcium. They also contain omega-3 acids which give birth to good cholesterol. Almonds are available throughout the year.

Almonds are a rich source of Vitamin E. 28 grams of almonds per day gives you a day's requirement of Vitamin E to the body.

The nut is a rich source of antioxidants which protects the body against free radicals that can harm cells in the body giving rise to chronic and dreadful diseases like stroke, heart attack, cancer etc.

Vitamin E contained in the nuts is known as the rejuvenating nut with anti-ageing effects. It can be eaten by itself or used in different recipes to keep the body in optimum levels of health.

According to researches at Tuffs University USA, 28 grams of almonds can provide an individual with heart friendly monounsaturated fat, Vitamin E, proteins, fibre, potassium, magnesium and iron and fibre.

Heat in the body: Almonds are one of the best nuts to beat the scorching heat of the summer. So in summer you should take 2 almonds which should be soaked over night in milk, peeled and taken with 1 cup milk daily to keep the body cool.

Start the day with almond sheera or almond milk shake which is not only healthy but also provides you with right calories and energy to start the day

For softening the skin: Mix together 1 egg yolk, 1 tablespoon powder of brewers yeast tablets and 1 teaspoon almond oil. Apply on the face and wash off with ordinary water after 20 minutes.

Softening bath powder: Mix together 3 tablespoons of oatmeal powder, 1 tablespoon oatmeal barn, 5 tablespoons ground almonds, and 1 teaspoon wheat flour. Add a few drops of perfume of your choice. Mix well and store in a jar. Use 1 tablespoon of this mixture in your bath water to have a soft and smooth skin.

Improving memory: Mix together 10 tulsi leaves, 4 almonds, 4 peppercorns and 1 teaspoon of honey. Take everyday in empty stomach to improve the memory.

Strengthening the brain: Soak 5 almonds whole night in water. Next morning peel and eat the almonds in empty stomach. After this, drink a glass of milk sweetened with 2 tablespoons of honey. This is very good for improving brain power and should be taken regularly by students.

Face wash: Apply almond powder mixed with milk and a pinch of turmeric powder. After 10 minutes, wash off with ordinary water. This removes dead cells and whitens and brightens the skin.

Almonds are high in monounsaturated fats and Vitamin E and so they are heart healthy; besides the nut contains a fair amount of magnesium which keeps the arteries and veins healthy. Almonds contain potassium which regulates the body pressure and keeps the blood pressure normal.

Almonds should be eaten with their skin to get the maximum benefit from the nut. To get instant energy just eat 28 grams of almonds everyday. These nuts are chock full of nutrients and vitamins. Therefore, they energise the body. If you kick start the day with almond shake you will feel on top of the world throughout the day. Take a glass of orange juice, 2 cups mixed fruits of your choice, 4 tablespoons of chopped almonds, 1 tablespoon of wheat germ, 2 table spoons honey and 60 grams tofu. Mix in the blender till smooth and have for breakfast.

Cashew nuts

Cashew nuts are the seeds of a tree that is native to Africa and South America. This kidney shaped nut grows in a double shell at the top of yellow pea-shaped fruit. These nuts are always sold shelled because their shells contain a caustic oil which is harmful to human body. Therefore, the nuts are very carefully removed from their shells to avoid contamination with this oil.

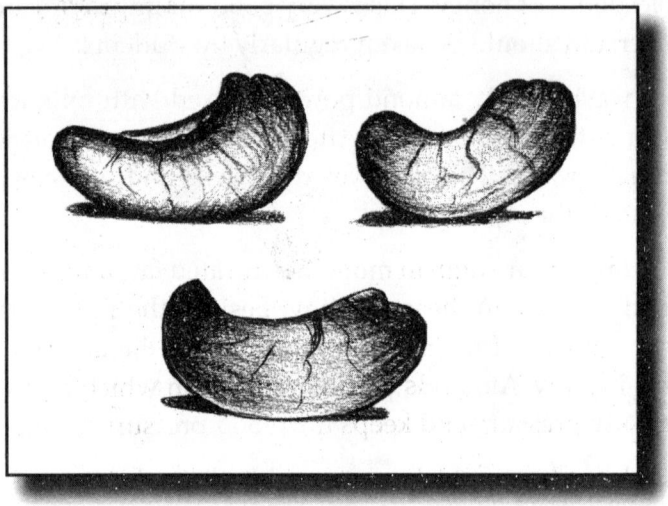

Cashew nuts are rich in saturated fats, folic acid, iron and B vitamins especially thiamine which not only helps combat depression but also rejuvenates the nervous system and stimulates the appetite. Riboflavin in the nut keeps the body active and energetic throughout the day.

Cashew nuts have lower calories than walnuts and almonds. They are rich in dietary fibre since they are low in glycaemic index they keep the stomach for a longer period of time.

Heart disease: They are rich sources of mono-unsaturated fats which contribute to good heart health.

Constipation: 20 cashew nuts eaten with 20 raisins daily helps remove constipation.

Leprosy: 12 roasted cashew nuts eaten with 5 flakes of garlic regularly produces remarkable changes in this disease. The nodules also start disappearing.

Warts: Oil of cashew nut kernel if applied on the skin diseases like warts, corns, ulcers, psoriasis and ringworm helps to cure them.

Anaemia: 20 cashew nuts eaten daily cures anaemia since they are rich in iron; 20 cashew nuts are just 100 calories.

Weakness in the legs: Grind a few cashew nuts in milk and massage into the legs to get relief.

Eating cashew nuts regularly prevents the onset of old age and prolongs youth. Cashew nuts increase cholesterol in the blood. So they should be eaten in small quantities by patients of diabetes, liver disorders, gastric ulcers, hypertension and urinary stones.

Raisin

Raisins are made by dried grapes. When grapes turn dry they have wrinkled skin which tastes as sweet as sugar. While the colour of raisins vary, they are usually of deep brown colour and the bigger raisins are of jet black colour which are known as munukka (in Hindi). Raisins are an ancient fruit which has a mention even in the first testament. The largest producer of raisins is California which is in USA. The story goes that in 1873, a strong heat wave destroyed the grape harvest by drying the grapes into raisins and one of the enterprising farmers started selling these raisins. To his surprise he received a very good response and this encourages him to convert grapes into raisins. Seeing his popularity many farmers followed this and raisins became a fast selling item throughout the world. Very soon everyone was hankering after this delicacy.

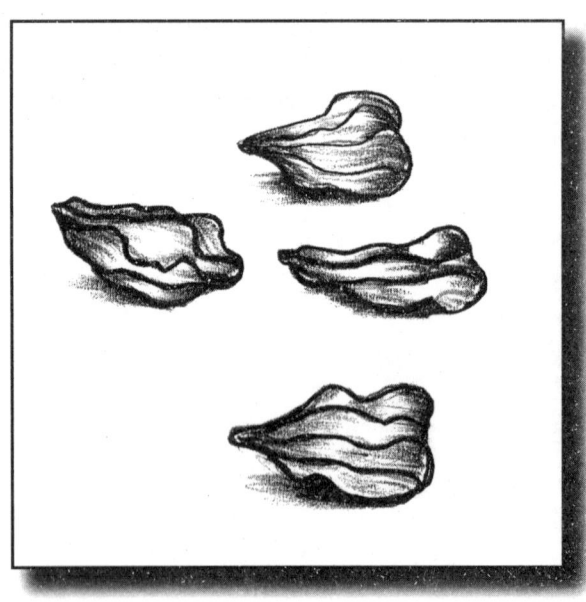

Oral health: Despite being sugary in taste, raisins do not harm the teeth. In fact, they promote oral health. Oleanolic acid a major component of raisins is very effective in killing the bacteria which causes tooth cavities and other diseases of the teeth.

Osteoporosis: Boron, an ingredient found in raisins provides protection against this disease.

Post menopausal problems: Raisins reproduce many of the positive effects of estrogen therapy in post menopausal women.

Vision disease: 25 raisins eaten per day will not only keep your eyes in excellent condition but will also help in destroying all vision problems. They also protect the cells from being destroyed.

Acidity: 12 raisins soaked in the water overnight and eaten first thing in the morning, reduces acidity and keeps the body cool.

Black grapes or munnuka soaked in the night in water and eaten in the morning cures anaemia since they are a rich source of iron. To get good results 12 to 15 raisins should be eaten each day.

Walnuts

Walnuts are shaped like human brain. They are the very good for keeping the brain in good order. They are the very sources of proteins which are easily digestible. They are also rich in unsaturated fatty acids, potassium, calcium, magnesium, phosphorus, carbohydrates, sulphur and B vitamins. Once the walnuts are shelled, they have no shelf life therefore they should always remain in the shell.

Blood vessels: This nut contains an amino acid arginine. The body uses to produce nitric acid which is of great importance to keep the body cells flexible.

Heart: This nut is very heart and brain friendly and also good for hair and skin because it contains Vitamin B, magnesium and important antioxidants which are excellent to keep these organs in optimum health condition.

Brain: Is an ideal brain food which improves memory and keeps the mind totally in control

Inflammatory skin diseases: Since the nut is rich in omega-3 fatty acids it helps in asthma, rheumatoid arthritis, inflammatory skin diseases such as eczema and psoriasis. This nut also reduces bad cholesterol and increases good cholesterol. It is a very powerful anti oxidant which fights free radicals.

Rheumatism: 12 walnuts eaten daily helps in curing this disease.

Warts: Rubbing juice of green walnuts on warts and ringworms cures this skin condition.

Brain weakness: Walnuts eaten with figs and raisins removes weakness of the brain.

Natural hair dye: Walnut shells which are fresh and green make an excellent hair dye for hair. Pound the green shells and cover them with water. Add a pinch of salt, cover and set aside for 3 days. After 3 days, put in 3 cups of boiling water and cook over a slow fire for 4 hours. As the water evaporates, add fresh water, when you see a dark liquid, remove from fire and strain through a cloth. Put the liquid back on fire and boil till it is reduced to about one-fourth its original quantity. Mix in a little glycerine and powdered alum. In the beginning when you apply it, it will produce a yellowish effect on the hair. But finally after some applications, it will give the hair a deep black colour and at the same time make the hair shiny, soft and manageable.

Walnuts are excellent for reducing the effects of dangerous fats on the blood vessels. After having a food rich in fat, if you finish it by eating some walnuts, this nut will help the onset of dangerous inflammation and oxidation of the arteries.

The nut also helps the arteries to maintain their flexibility even in patients suffering from high choles treating.

10 to 12 walnuts per day will keep you healthy; prevent heart disease and other diseases; put a glow in your skin and hair and keep you youthful for a long, long time.

Pistachios

Pistachios have very great nutritional value. It is also having mention in the Bible! It is a nut which is coming down to human beings since centuries to bestow its goodness on mankind. They are very delicious in taste and are rich sources of iron, protein and calcium.

Since it is rich in iron, it increases red blood cells and destroys anaemia. It also assists in the process of respiration.

Cholesterol: Since this nut has mono unsaturated fats, it lowers bad cholesterol.

They are a low glycemic index food and so can easily be eaten by diabetics and obese people.

Diabetes: This nut helps maintain blood sugar levels therefore makes it ideal for diabetics.

Cataracts: This nut contains the antioxidant lutien which reduces the risk of cataract and other age related diseases. It lowers blood lipid levels and increases antioxidants in the blood.

It also helps in toothache and cirrhosis of liver.

Since this nut is rich in potassium it helps balance the body's liquid levels.

Since it is high in B vitamins, it helps in protein metabolism and absorption, compared to other nuts. This nut is low in calories and it also reduces the risk of developing cancer and heart disease. It is known to be the highest antioxidant nut, most nutritious and contains the highest fibre content amongst nuts. It contains lowest calories and lowest fat amongst nuts and gives the highest nutrition benefits to the body.

This nut is high in monounsaturated fats and proteins and so you should not eat more than 30 nuts per week.

Ground nut

Despite its name it is not a nut it is a legume and it belongs to the bean family. It is an economical source of proteins and is rich in monounsaturated fat and also contains useful amounts of potassium, thiamine, niacin, Vitamin E, phosphorus, magnesium, copper selenium and zinc. This nut also is rich in flavonoids and anti-oxidants

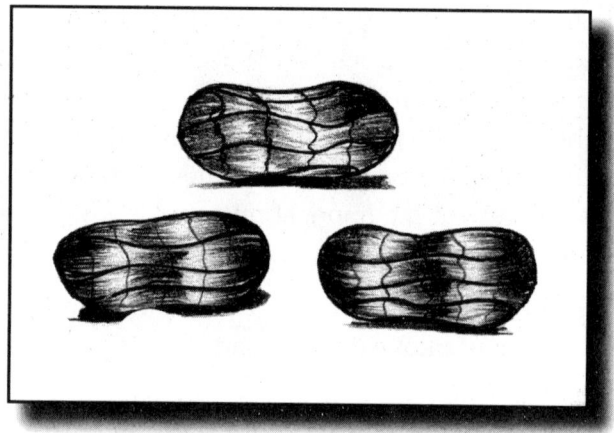

Heart: Recent research has shown that ground nuts reduce the incidence of heart disease if taken regularly. They are especially beneficial in reducing palpitation of the heart; this nut also helps in reducing bad cholesterol.

Diabetes: 20 to 40 nuts consumed daily checks the development of vascular complications in diabetics. This nut reduces the risk of type-2 diabetes in women if they eat ground nuts daily.

Weight management: Since these nuts have high satiety value they will keep you full for longer periods. This checks the desire to over eat; therefore this nut helps in managing your weight.

Teeth: Chewing fresh ground nuts with a pinch of salt kills harmful bacteria and safe guards the enamel of the teeth.

Dry skin: 1 teaspoon of ground nut oil mixed with equal quantity of lime juice applied in the night before going to bed in the night checks dryness of the skin and makes the skin soft and smooth.

Ground nuts should be avoided by patients suffering from asthma, jaundice and gastric problems. Over eating these nuts can cause indigestion and burning in the chest. Since these nuts can cause choking in the throat, children and old people should be given powder of these nuts or the nuts should be chopped finely before giving it to them to be on the safer side

Ground nuts are high in fibre and fatty acids. Therefore they give protection against heart diseases.

Coconut

Coconut is considered very auspicious. It is the only nut which is offered at every temple to all the deities. Each and every portion of the nut is helpful to the human body whether its water inside, flesh or its outer skin.

Coconut water is full of nutrients such as sodium, potassium, calcium, magnesium, iron, copper, phosphorus, sulphur, chlorine and B vitamins. Only fresh water of green coconut contains most of the above mentioned vitamins and minerals but as the coconut dries most of its nutrients are lost so you should only drink water of fresh coconut and you should drink it immediately after opening the nut; otherwise its water will loses its potency.

It is very useful in diabetics and since it is diuretic. It provides relief in kidney stones, retention of urine, burning in the urinary tract and other diseases of the urinary tracts.

It also provides relief in cholera because the body gets dehydrated due to vomiting and diarrhoea.

Coconut water helps in cholera because it removes dehydration by providing necessary salts and water to the body. Besides it removes the germs of cholera from the body as it is anti-bacterial.

Eyes and ears: If grated coconut is eaten with sugar candy it proves a real tonic to all the organs of the body especially to the eyes, ears and brain. This mixture is also excellent for the baby in the womb because it makes the baby grow healthy and beautiful of eaten daily by a pregnant woman.

Pain and swelling: Take coconut paste and mix it with turmeric powder. Heat it and foment the painful areas with this to get relief from pain and swelling.

Headache: To remove headache massage the head with warm coconut oil.

Worms: Drinking coconut water daily expels the worms from the intestines. Coconut water taken daily with its flesh during pregnancy ensures plenty of breast milk.

Leprosy: Massage the painful areas with warm coconut oil mixed with little turmeric powder to get relief.

Insomnia: Eat 2 tablespoons of shredded coconut with 1 tablespoon of honey and drink a cup of hot milk over it to get a good night's sleep.

Coconut is an excellent food for eyes and the brain. If it is eaten with sugar, it not only proves a real tonic for the eyes and the brain but to all the organs of the body.

Mixture of coconut and sugar candy is also good for the unborn baby which grows healthy and beautiful if eaten by a pregnant woman daily.

Flax Seeds

Seeds along with nuts curb hunger in the body. Flax seeds are very essential for the body because they contain omega-3 fatty acids which not only balances the hormones in the body, but also helps strengthening hair and skin.

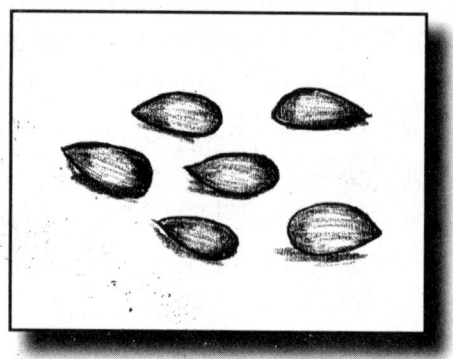

Flavonoids in flax seeds help in lowering cholesterol and cause the cancer cells mutate.

Menstrual cramps are caused by prostaglandin production. The uterus reacts to prostaglandin released into the tissues and goes into spasms. But flax seeds can inhibit the release of prostaglandin and cure the body of menstrual spasms. Take 2 teaspoons of ground flax seeds daily to be cured of your problems. Flax seeds are rich sources of omega-3 fatty acids which inhibit heart attacks. So people who are vegetarians or who do not like eating fish should take flax seeds in powdered form daily.

Since it is very rich in omega-3 fatty acids, it enhances the mechanical performance and electrical stability of the heart. It is also useful in the treatment of inflammation, arthritis, constipation and dry eyes. It can be eaten in a powdered form mixed with water, milk, cereal or flour.

CHAPTER 6

Dairy Products

Milk

Milk is called the 'nectar of the earth'. It is said in Indian mythology that even Lord Krishna loved milk. In all the Hindu religious ceremonies, milk is an important item of food which is used in the worship of God. No religious ceremony is complete without the use of milk. It is an integral part in the worship of the all great Indian deities like Lord Shiva and Lord Krishna. So, milk is held in the highest esteem in India. Milk is considered to be a complete food because it contains all the essential nutrients required for maintaining a healthy body.

Healing Powers of Milk

Acidity: Milk's calcium content and other mineral salts checks the acidity in the stomach.

Thinness: Milk increases weight. Milk made into a milk shake with 1 ripe banana and 1 egg if taken daily first thing in the morning increases bodily weight by forming new muscle tissues. Consuming a glass of milk daily also improves the blood circulation and improves a weak pulse, does away with wrinkles and puts a shine in the skin and the eyes.

Hypertension: Since milk is full of calcium, if taken regularly it helps in lowering blood pressure.

Calming the nerves: Since milk is a rich source of calcium it calms the nerves if taken daily.

Insomnia: A glass of milk mixed with 2 tablespoons of honey if taken before going to sleep gives you a sound sleep.

Pain and burning whilst passing urine: Drink 1 cup water mixed with half cup of milk and 2 teaspoons juice of tulsi to get relief.

Internal or external wounds: 1 glass of hot milk with ¼ teaspoon of turmeric powder mixed, cures both internal and external wounds.

Piles: Ripe banana if taken with milk cures piles.

Stoppage of urine: 1 cup milk mixed with 1 cup water and a teaspoon of rose water starts the flow of urine immediately.

Burns: If cold milk is applied immediately on a burn, it will heal fast without leaving scars.

Weeping blisters: Make a solution by mixing 1/2 teaspoon of salt dissolved in 1 cup of milk. Then apply a cloth, wet with this solution on the weeping blisters to get relief.

Milk pack: Damp some cotton wool with milk and clean the face with it. The skin will become clean, soft and glowing if you use this daily on the face.

Cleansing pack: Take 1 tablespoon each of gram flour and orange peel powder. Mix with 2 tablespoons of cream (found on top of boiled and cooled milk) and apply on the face evenly. Remove with a piece of cotton wool and wash off with plain water. This will make the skin clean, soft and smooth.

Skin tightening pack: Take 2 tablespoons starch and mix with 2 tablespoons of warm milk. Apply on the face and keep for 15 minutes. Then wash off with plain water. This keeps the skin firm and smooth.

Dead skin remover: Mix together 1 tablespoon ground almonds with 1 tablespoon of cream (found on top of boiled and cooled milk). Rub on the face in an upward movement and then wash off with plain water.

Common cold: Boil 1 glass of milk with ½ teaspoon turmeric powder and 1 teaspoon of cumin seeds. Sip whilst hot to get relief.

Soft skin: To maintain a soft and smooth skin, dip a piece of cotton wool in cold milk to which add a pinch of turmeric. Pat all over the face and wash off after half an hour.

Lightening the complexion: Mix a teaspoon of ground almonds in 1 tablespoon of cold milk and 1 teaspoon honey. Apply on the face and leave for half an hour then wash off with plain water.

To brighten a dull complexion: Mix 2 tablespoons of milk powder with enough hydrogen peroxide to form a paste. Mix in a few drops of liquid ammonia. Apply for 10 minutes on the face and then wash off with plain water.

Dark and dull complexion: To improve a dark and dull complexion, soak a tablespoon of gram in a little milk for a whole night. Next morning, grind to a paste and mix in a pinch of turmeric powder and add a few drops of lime juice. Apply on the face and wash off after 20 minutes.

For a bright complexion: To brighten the complexion, take 1 tablespoon of milk and mix in 1 teaspoon of each— carrot, orange juice and honey. Leave it on for 15 minutes and then wash off with plain water.

Dry skin: Take a tablespoon of gram flour and mix in a pinch of turmeric powder, 1/4 teaspoon of orange peel powder and 1 teaspoon each of curds and milk. Apply on the skin and when the skin starts feeling taut, rub the skin with your hands in the upward direction till it glows. Then wash off with plain water.

Skin pigmentation: Fry a teaspoon of red lentil in 1 teaspoon of olive oil to a red colour. Grind to a paste and add a few drops of lime juice and honey. Apply on the face and keep for 15 minutes. Wash off with plain water.

Itching: To get relieve from itching, grind 1 teaspoon of yellow mustard to a paste and mix with 1 tablespoon milk. Apply on the itching portions of the skin for half an hour and then wash off with plain water.

Rough skin: Take 2 tablespoons of cream (found on top of boiled and cooled milk). Add a teaspoon of almond oil and a few drops rose water. Apply on the rough skin and wash off with plain water after half an hour.

Hydrating and nutritious bath: Mix together 2 cups milk, 1/2 cup honey and 2 tablespoons each of olive oil, honey and rose water. Put in a tub of warm water and bathe in it for half an hour or so. This, not only hydrates the skin but also makes it glow and shine.

Blemished skin: Grate an apple and mix in 1 tablespoon milk and apply on the skin. Leave it on for 15 minutes and then wash off with plain water. This softens and lightens the blemishes on the skin.

Dark circles under the eyes: Mash a ripe banana and mix with 1 teaspoon of each of milk and honey. Apply on the face and wash off after 15 minutes. This not only removes dark circles but also removes wrinkles from the face and makes it wrinkle free.

Greasy skin: Pour milk in an ice tray and keep in the freezer. When ever you go out just rub the cube on the face and your face will not only look fresh and alive but the skin will also be rejuvenated.

Skin tightener: Mash 2 strawberries and mix in 1 teaspoon each of oatmeal powder, milk and cucumber juice. Apply on the face for 20 minutes and then wash off with plain water.

At bedtime, if you drink a glass of milk it will induce good sleep. It will give you enough calcium to maintain healthy bones and teeth. For those who have an early dinner, a glass of hot milk will not only curb your hunger pangs but will also give you a good sleep.

For whitening and brightening the skin: In 1 tablespoon of hydrogen peroxide add a teaspoon of milk powder and a few drops of liquid ammonia. Apply on the face keeping the paste well away from the eyes. After 15 minutes wash off with plain water. This will not only whiten the face but also brighten it. This also bleaches fine hair on the face.

Dry hair: An excellent cleanser for dry hair is to beat an egg in a cup of milk, rub into the scalp, leave on for 5 minutes and then wash off with a mild shampoo. Do this twice a week to improve the condition of the hair.

Curd

Curd is held in high esteem for its smoothness and its pleasant and refreshing taste. It is highly versatile, health promoting and one of the most valuable therapeutic foods. In a study reported from New York Times, it has been reported that curds prevent heart attacks by lowering cholesterol in the blood.

Cholesterol is a fatty substance which is notorious for its ability to clog the arteries of the heart leading to a heart disease which is known as arteriosclerosis. According to a study conducted by Dr Mann of the African Medical Research Foundation, curd brings about a dramatic decline in the body's own production of cholesterol. Dr Mann believes that the bacteria in the curd produces a substance that blocks the cholesterol formation in the liver.

Curd is a valuable source of proteins, vitamins and essential minerals. The protein in curd is more easily digestible than milk. It makes an ideal diet for those with sensitive digestive systems especially small children and elderly people.

In the process of making curds, certain bacteria enter the curd. This friendly bacteria then inhibits the growth of disease causing bacteria inside the intestinal tract and promotes beneficial bacteria which is needed for the digestion of food. This friendly bacteria facilitates the absorption of minerals and vitamins of B group. Buttermilk is a by product of curd. It has the same curative value as curds; it is rich in proteins, calcium and B Vitamins.

These days probiotic curd is being widely sold in the market. Probiotic refers to friendly bacteria which are given via food to the body. During every illness the first thing that gets disturbed is the balance of good and bad bacteria in the body. The bad bacterium interferes with digestion and negates the good effects of the friendly bacteria. Consuming probiotic foods brings back the level of good and bad bacteria to normal and helps the body to recover faster from disease.

Stomach ailments: Probiotic curds help cure all the stomach related diseases. The bacteria creates a friendly atmosphere which helps the stomach secrete a better quality of fatty acid which helps in the digestion of food.

Heart friendly: Probiotic curds favour the growth of short chain fatty acids in the large intestines which bring down the cholesterol in the blood thus reducing the chances of heart ailments.

Antibiotic effects: When you take antibiotics to kill bad bacteria, along with these bacteria, the antibiotics also kills the friendly bacteria. Probiotic curds push the level back to normal and thereby neutralizing the bad effects of antibiotics on the body.

Diarrhoea and dysentery: The bacteria which cause diarrhoea and dysentery cannot thrive in the presence of lactic acid found in curd and buttermilk. Therefore, curd and buttermilk not only cures these two diseases but also helps in appendicitis, colitis, constipation and gastric ulcers.

Insomnia: Buttermilk taken with honey after dinner promotes a good sleep. It also promotes longevity. Our body is often poisoned and its resistance is weakened by unhealthy diet which consists of junk food and highly spiced and fried foods. This food creates toxins in the body. This poisoning process can be arrested and the intestinal tract can be kept healthy by the regular use of curd and buttermilk.

Piles: Curd should be mixed with rice along with grated ginger and eaten daily to get relief.

Appetizer: Buttermilk taken with rock salt and powdered cumin seeds acts as an appetizer.

Burning sensation in the throat: If curd is eaten with sugar, it not only removes the burning sensation in the throat, but also acts as a thirst quencher.

Baldness: Put curd in a copper vessel. When it turns green, apply on the bald spots and leave for a few hours and then wash off. Hair will grow back within a short time.

Boils in the head: Mix curd with mustard oil and apply on the head. Leave on for half an hour then wash off.

Dandruff: Massage the scalp with curd and wash off after 1 hour to get relief.

Mouth ulcers: Mix curd with honey and apply on the mouth ulcers a few times daily to be cured.

Skin pigmentation: Mix 1 tablespoon of curd with ½ teaspoon each of gram flour, orange peel powder, mustard oil and lime juice. Apply on the skin and wash off after half an hour. This reduces pigmentation.

Buttermilk: Buttermilk is the best home remedy for curing diarrhoea. It is the residual milk left after the fat is removed from the curd after churning it. Buttermilk helps to destroy the bacteria in the intestines. The acid in the buttermilk helps in fighting the disease forming bacteria. Buttermilk should be taken with a pinch of black salt three or four times per day to get relief from this disease.

CHAPTER 7

Honey

Honey is known as the 'nectar of Gods' because honey is a chock-full of nutrients and has numerous medicinal qualities. It is composed of fructose, glucose and water in varying proportions. Apart from this, it contains traces of iron, copper, silica, manganese, chlorine, calcium, potassium, sodium, phosphorus, sulphur and aluminum.

Benefits of Honey

Honey is an excellent source of energy. It creates and replenishes energy and forms tissues in the body. It also promotes oxidation. It is an antioxidant, anti-microbial and has wound healing properties. Honey helps in asthma, gives relief in cough, cold, aids and digestion.

Light coloured honey is usually better than the dark coloured honey. Daily use of honey strengthens the immune system and protects the body from bacterial and viral attacks.

According to a recent research regular use of honey strengthens the white blood corpuscles to fight disease. Packed with health and power, honey can be used in many diseases.

Healing Powers of Honey

Asthma: It is extremely beneficial for asthma patients. It not only provides warmth to the body but also dissolves phlegm in the respiratory tract. A mixture of 1 cup warm water with 2 tablespoons of honey and ¼ teaspoon of pepper powder if taken daily will delay the onset of an asthmatic attack by half an hour giving ample opportunity to get medical help. Another good remedy is to drink 2 tablespoons of honey with 6 tulsi leaves and 6 peppercorns.

Upset stomach: Take a glass of warm water and add 1 tablespoon of cider vinegar and honey and sip slowly to relieve pain.

Indigestion: Make a solution with 1 tablespoon of cider vinegar and 1 tablespoon of honey. Swallow a teaspoon and then slowly sip a glass of warm water. Do this 3 to 4 times in a day to get relief.

Acidity: Mix 1 teaspoon of honey in half cup of warm water and sip slowly.

Fatigue: Put 1 teaspoon each of honey and cider vinegar in half glass water and drink slowly to get relief.

Chronic fatigue: Mix 2 teaspoons of cider vinegar in 1 cup honey. Place in the fridge. Take 2 teaspoons every night before going to.

Painful piles: Drink 1 cup of apple juice mixed with 1 teaspoon of honey to get relief daily.

Toothache: Make a paste of 1 tablespoon honey and 1 teaspoon of cinnamon powder. Rub on the aching tooth thrice a day till you are relieved.

Bladder infection: Dissolve 1 tablespoon of cinnamon powder and 1 teaspoon of honey in a glass of hot water and sip slowly.

Cholesterol: Dissolve 1 teaspoon each of honey and cinnamon powder in 1 cup of green tea and drink slowly. This reduces cholesterol in the blood.

Infertility: Take 2 tablespoons of honey before going to bed at night. This cures infertility in men. Women who cannot conceive should take half teaspoon of cinnamon powder mixed in 1 tablespoon honey regularly.

Heart disease: Make a paste of 2 tablespoons of honey and 1 teaspoon of cinnamon powder. Eat regularly before breakfast. This reduces cholesterol in the arteries and prevents heart attack, regularizes breathing and heart beats.

Flu: Taking 2 teaspoons of honey regularly in empty stomach can kill influenza germs and save you from flu.

Insomnia: Mix 2 tablespoons of honey in your bath water and keep it for 20 minutes before bathing. This will provide you with a good sleep at night.

Depression: Mix 1 glass of milk with grated apple and 1 tablespoon of honey. This is a very effective tonic for depression and for recharging the nerves with new life and energy.

Burns: Apply honey immediately on the burns to prevent blistering. It cures burnt skin leaving no marks behind.

Vomiting: To prevent vomiting, mix together 1 tablespoon each of honey and pomegranate juice and take this mixture twice daily.

Burning in the chest: Mix together 1 teaspoon each of lime juice and honey and take twice daily. This not only stops burning in the chest but accumulation of saliva in the mouth too.

Painful tonsils: In 1 glass of warm water, mix the juice of 1 lime, 1 teaspoon honey and ¼ teaspoon of salt; sip slowly to get relief.

Scanty menses: Take 1 teaspoon each of ginger and mint juice with 1 tablespoon of honey twice daily; once in the morning and once in the evening.

Blood purifier: Take a glass of grape juice and mix in a pinch of asafoetida and 2 tablespoons honey. This is an excellent blood purifier which should be taken daily.

Pain in the throat: Take 1 teaspoon of honey and the pain will vanish immediately.

Children who take a tablespoon of honey regularly, increase their weight and energy. Honey also cures anaemia in anaemic children by increasing their blood count.

2 tablespoons of honey contain as much energy as 1 large egg. Therefore, it makes an excellent supplement for people who suffer from debilitating diseases.

Flu and cold: One teaspoon of honey added to ½ cup pomegranate juice helps in curing this disease.

Reduction in weight: A tablespoon of honey mixed with 1 teaspoon of lime juice taken daily not only reduces the weight and also keeps the body slim and trim.

Cystitis: 1 teaspoon of honey mixed with 1 teaspoon of lime juice taken in 3 tablespoons of hot water every two hours will stop burning and bleeding in this disease.

Honey and Beauty—an Inextricable Relation

Oily skin: Take 1 tablespoon of tomato juice, 1 teaspoon honey and put in a few drops of camphor. Apply on the skin and leave it on for 15 minutes and then wash off. This will help reduce the oil in the skin.

Dead skin: Apply 1 teaspoon honey mixed with 2 teaspoons of cream found on the top of boiled and cooled milk on the face. Remove after 15 minutes with plain water.

Dry skin: Mash half a ripe banana and mix with 1 teaspoon of honey and 2 teaspoons of cream found on the top of boiled and cooled milk. Apply on the face and keep for 20 minutes and then wash off with plain water.

Greasy skin: In a half a mashed ripe banana, mix in 1 tablespoon of orange juice and 1 teaspoon of honey.

Apply on the face and wash off with plain water after 20 minutes.

Hair conditioner: Mix together 1 egg, 1 teaspoon of honey and 2 tablespoons of olive oil. Massage into the scalp and shampoo after half an hour with a mild shampoo. This will make the hair soft and manageable.

Exfoliating mask: Take steam on the face for 5 minutes. Then smear warm honey mixed with powdered almonds on the face. Leave on for 15 minutes then wash off with plain water and then splash on rose water. This is an excellent exfoliating mask.

Sugar, Jaggery and Salt

Sugar

Although, sugar and salt are considered to be white poisons especially for people who are suffering from diabetes, hypertension heart and kidney problems, but these two are important ingredients of our daily meals. They are life saving in certain cases of medical emergencies.

Weak heart: If 4 tablespoons of pomegranate seeds are eaten with 1 tablespoon sugar, it strengthens the heart.

Hypoglycemia or low blood sugar: In 1 glass of water or milk, mix in 1 tablespoon of sugar and drink it to get quick relief. A diabetic should always carry sugar with him where ever he goes.

For putting on weight: In 1 glass of milk, mix in 1 ripe chickoo and ½ ripe banana and 2 tablespoons of sugar and take daily in the morning before eating anything to put on weight.

Cold: Fill a jar with dry raspberries and cover them to the top of the jar with sugar lumps. Set aside till the sugar melts. In the initial stages of cold, put 1 tablespoon of the syrup in a glass of hot water and drink. The cold will be cured immediately.

Heat in the body: Fill a jar with sweet smelling rose petals layered with sugar. The sugar should reach the top of the jar. Seal tightly and keep in the sun for 20 days. After this, it will turn into glucand. This glucand if taken daily will keep the body cool especially in the warm weather and also rejuvenate the body. To get the best benefits, take a tablespoon of glucand with 1 glass milk in empty stomach.

Diarrhoea: In 1 glass of water add a teaspoon of sugar and a pinch of salt if you are suffering from diarrhoea and vomiting. Drink this a few times in a day to prevent dehydration.

Spotty skin: Dissolve 1 tablespoon of sugar in a glass of water and wash your face with this mixture to improve the complexion.

Sugarcane juice from which sugar is processed is the purest form of sugar. The juice is rich in glucose which is used by muscles in the body as a source of energy. Therefore, a glass of sugarcane juice is a great energy booster. Sugarcane juice helps in prostrate and breast cancer. It should be taken mixed with lime juice and ginger juice for better results.

Salt

Salts come in different varieties. The common variety is iodised salt which contains iodine which easily dissolves in the dish. And then, there is the sea salt that doesn't have iodine which comes in chunks that crunch beneath the teeth. Sometimes it comes in delicate flakes which dissolve on the tongue. Here we will talk about table salt.

Sore throat: Mix 2 tablespoons of bicarbonate of soda with 1 tablespoon of salt in a glass of hot water and gargle with it for 2 to 3 times daily to get relief. A small quantity of water should be also swallowed for better results.

Itching: Take 1 tablespoon of bicarbonate of soda. Add a pinch of salt and make a paste with rose water and apply on the part which is itching to get relief.

Low blood pressure: In 1 glass water, add 1 tablespoon of sugar and 1/8 teaspoon of salt. Drink this to get relief.

Yellow or stained teeth: Rub the teeth with lime juice mixed with salt twice a week to whiten the teeth.

Indigestion: Take 1 teaspoon of thymol/carom seeds mixed with a pinch of black salt with water to get immediate relief from indigestion.

Bleeding gums: Massage the gums regularly with a little mustard oil mixed with salt.

Dull face: Apply on the face, 4 teaspoons of milk mixed with ¼ teaspoon of salt. Wash off after 15 minutes. This puts a glow on the dull skin.

Vomiting: To induce vomiting in case of poisoning add 1 teaspoon of salt in 1 glass water and make the patient drink. 2 teaspoons of salt in a glass of lukewarm water is a good emetic. Gargling with half teaspoonful of salt in a glass of warm water helps in relieving pain in the throat.

Dark skin: Mix grated apple with a pinch of salt. Apply on the face and wash off after half an hour. Apply this regularly to get a fairer skin.

Headache due to migraine: Eat an apple with a pinch of salt for 7 days in empty stomach to be cured of this problem.

Aphrodisiac-Rock salt is not only considered excellent for boosting your sex life but it is also good tonic for the heart.

CHAPTER 8

Vegetables

Vegetables and fruits are chock-full of vitamins and minerals. In general this category may have green leafy vegetables like spinach, asparagus, broccoli, spinach, fenugreek, mustard greens, cabbage etc. contain plenty of life giving vitamins and minerals like riboflavin, Vitamin C, folacin, potassium and calcium.

Benefits of Vegetables

All types of vegetables supply the body with natural sugars which provide energy to the body; besides, they supply fibre to the body. When eaten raw, juices of vegetables are very nutritious.

Lime and amla juices are full of Vitamin C which is required for maintenance of healthy skin, hair nails and teeth. Cucumber juice prevents water retention in the body and therefore prevents a bloated look. Juices of green vegetables prevent anaemia and therefore provide a rosy look to the skin.

The greener the vegetable the higher is the Vitamin A content of the vegetable and because of the calcium and riboflavin content in green vegetables they should be eaten in higher quantities by people who are allergic to milk.

Their Vitamin C content compares favourably with citrus fruits like oranges and lime. The bulbs, roots and tubers contribute calories to the body. 1 cup of carrot or beet root has 50 calories; 1 medium potato contains 100 calories and 1 medium sweet potato has 150 calories.

Vitamin C improves the quality of the skin. This vitamin forms collagen in the body. Collagen is the key element of the connective tissue that keeps the skin firm, smooth and glowing. It also builds the walls of the blood vessels and helps strengthening them which gives a more resilient skin.

Deep green and yellow vegetables like carrots, papayas and pumpkin contain Vitamin A which makes the skin soft, smooth as silk and keeps all ailments of the skin away. These vegetables and fruits contain beta carotene which in turn turns into Vitamin A after the food is digested. This vitamin is also excellent for eyes, ear and hair.

Fats found in fish like tuna, salmon and cods are of extreme importance for the maintenance of body health. Therefore, you should eat fish least 2 to 3 times a week. However, if you are a vegetarian you can eat instead of fish a teaspoon of flax seeds each day.

Proteins found in meat and other meat products should be eaten regularly because proteins are of great importance to the body. They build up and maintain the tissues in the body. The muscles, the various organs and even some of the hormones in the body are made of proteins.

Proteins make haemoglobin which is responsible for supplying oxygen to all the organs of the body. Proteins also make antibodies which fight free radicals and thus keep away infection and disease from the body. If you are a vegetarian then you can get your daily quota of proteins by including pulses, beans and nuts in your daily diet.

The fresher the vegetables the more nutrients they contain. Carotene which is converted into Vitamin A is an important vitamin found in the vegetables. It is very sensitive to oxygen. If carrots and other orange vegetables are chopped and kept for 20 minutes, they lose most of their Vitamin A content.

In the same way, if citrus fruits which contain the valuable Vitamin C are preserved for some time they start losing the vitamin. So, you should buy fresh and deep coloured vegetables and fruits so that they have greater vitamin content.

Vitamin C helps build collagen which keeps the skin young and removes toxins from the body.

All types of berries protect the skin against ageing because they contain antioxidants called phytochemicals. They provide inner clearness to the body thereby detoxifying it.

Broccoli and Cauliflower

Broccoli and cauliflower are both like sisters. They contain isothiocyanates which stimulates the liver to break down pesticides and cancer causing products in the body.

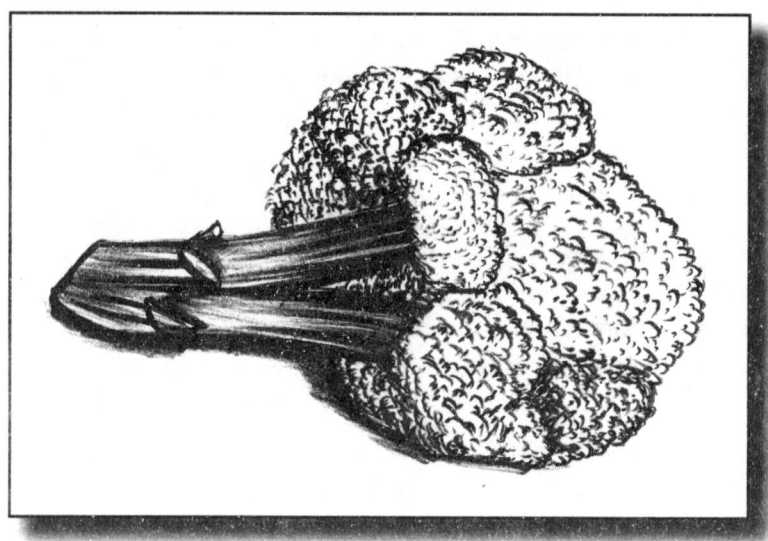

Benefits

Broccoli and cauliflower are cruciferous vegetables because their flowers are four petaled and they are rich in vitamin A and C, fibre, folic acid, iron and calcium.

Broccoli has one of the highest concentrations of sulphorephanes one of the most powerful phytochemicals which boost the production of anti-cancerous enzymes. It is one of the best foods along with cauliflower which boosts life.

The vegetable is rich in calcium. Therefore, it gives the body protection against osteoporosis. Its calcium is similar to that found in milk and dairy products. So, it strengthens teeth and bones.

It contains folic acid and is very important for pregnant women.

According to US national cancer institute the cruciferous vegetables like broccoli and cauliflower lower the risk of developing colon cancer.

Beetroot

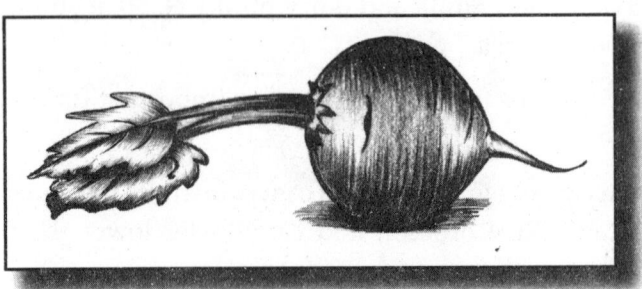

Benefits of Beetroot

Beetroot is a native of Mediterranean and is 2000 years old. It was the favourite food of the Romans and the Greeks. It contains carbohydrates, calcium, phosphorus, proteins and Vitamins B and C. Juice of beets prevents malignancy in the body and is an excellent food for cancer patients. Beet juice is an excellent food for those who want to gain weight. It cures anaemia and also cures weakness in the body.

Beetroot when eaten as a salad removes constipation by cleansing the stomach and the intestines.

Beets rich red colour contains powerful antioxidants which is very strong in fighting all types of cancers.

Beetroot is very essential to a pregnant woman for the normal growth of the baby. Besides, it acts against birth defects.

Beets should be eaten raw or in the form of juice or they should be cooked very lightly if you want to have the vegetables maximum benefit. Besides, its anti-cancer properties are destroyed when cooked.

Bitter Gourd

Benefits of Bitter gourd

Bitter gourd is bitter in taste and so not many people like this vegetable. But this is a vegetable which provide ample benefits to the body. Besides containing Vitamins A, B and C, it has traces of carbohydrates, calcium and phosphorus. It is an antioxidant because of Vitamins A and C.

A glass of bitter gourd juice taken in the morning in empty stomach not only benefits patients of jaundice but also gives relief to diabetics and those suffering from arthritis. The juice also cures cough, gas formation in the stomach, fever, worms, anaemia and leucoderma.

The vegetable purifies the blood. It provides relief in piles. It is an excellent diuretic and therefore relieves burning in the kidneys and also helps in dissolving kidney stones. It removes impurities from the blood and therefore is of great help in purifying the blood.

 # Drumstick

Drumstick is a very common vegetable in India, valued for its tender pods which are anti-bacterial and a wonderful cleanser. Almost all the parts of drumstick tree is used for medicinal purposes which helps the body fight disease.

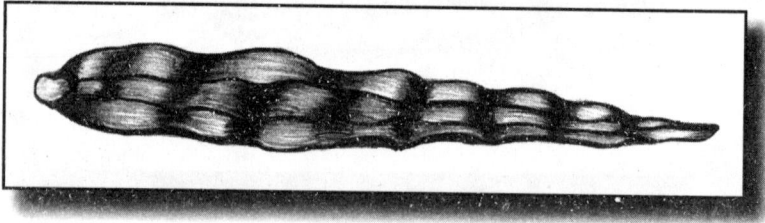

Benefits of Drumstick

The leaves of a drumstick tree if cooked and eaten provide calcium, iron and necessary vitamins to the expectant mothers and facilitates an easy delivery.

Drumsticks are beneficial in the treatment of TB, asthma and bronchitis. Drumsticks are rich in iron and therefore cure anaemia. Drumsticks also lower sugar in diabetics. Drumsticks are a rich source carotene, calcium and phosphorus. They have anti-bacterial properties akin to penicillin and therefore they not only kill free radicals, but also prevent disease from attacking the body.

Cucumber

Cucumber grows on vine and is usually eaten as a salad in its natural form. Cucumber is the coolest vegetable amongst all the vegetables and it is very good for eating it in summer because it reduces the body heat thus preventing the body from falling a victim to sun stroke.

Benefits of Cucumber

It is a rich source of Vitamin B, iron, phosphorus and has traces of calcium. Cucumber is an ideal food for reducing weight since its low in calories. Cucumber is also an excellent food for diabetics because of its low glycemic index. Cucumber cures all the diseases of the urinary tract. Cucumber helps in the treatment of rheumatism.

Cabbage

Benefits of Cabbage

Cabbage belongs to the category of green leafy vegetables. It is a very high source of Vitamin C. 1 cup of chopped raw cabbage provides the body with one-third amount of a day's allowance of this vitamin. The outer green leaves of cabbage contain high amounts of Viamin A besides containing the mineral iron and Vitamin B.

The cabbage should be cooked in minimum of water and in the minimum of time. Excessive cooking destroys its Vitamins B and C. The water in which it is cooked is full of nutrients like Vitamin C, calcium, iron, phosphorus and magnesium.

Vegetables

Cabbage is the only vegetable which contains Vitamin U which is a sure cure for gastric ulcers and peptic ulcers. It is called an anti-peptic ulcer.

1 cup of raw cabbage should be taken because the Vitamin U is destroyed in cooking. Taking 450 ml of cabbage juice at intervals of 5 hours everyday will remove pain in 5 days and the healing process will start from the fourteenth day onwards.

Cabbage is also found very effective in curing arthritis, pyorrhea, indigestion, vision disturbances and obesity. The isothiocyanates found in cabbage breaks down pesticides and other cancer causing products in the body. It is also useful for curing cough, leucoderma and impurities in the blood. Cabbage is low in calories which is the best food for reducers. A cup of cabbage contains only 20 calories. Cabbage is a great source of Vitamin A which contains natural chemicals that make our eyes age gracefully.

Carrot

Carrots were grown in Kashmir and western Himalayas but now it is grown all over India. Carrots are rich in vitamins A, B, carbohydrates, calcium, phosphorus, iron and proteins.

Benefits of Carrots

The carotene in carrots is converted into Vitamin A in the body and therefore it is an excellent food for maintaining the health of eyes, skin, ears and hair.

It is an excellent food for preventing diseases like fistula, dysentery, worms, cough and gastric troubles. It helps in eradicating and preventing these diseases.

Carrots contain a hormone cytokinin. This is like insulin like compound which is useful for diabetics. Carrots eaten with salt have proved beneficial in the treatment of eczema. Chewing raw carrots gives not only strength to the teeth but also helps in cleaning and brightening them. Carrots juice if taken regularly destroys harmful bacteria in the intestines and also heals intestinal ulcers. It helps in increasing the flow of urine when it is scanty and is an excellent medicine for nephritis. It destroys uric acid in the blood and therefore it is an excellent item of food for patient suffering from gout. Carrots contain the valuable Vitamin E. It destroys cancer cells and therefore it gives protection against this disease. It provides relief to patients suffering from liver diseases, tuberculosis, gall stones and scanty menses. Carrots are believed to contain an anti-sterility factor. Cabbage cures anaemia and is an excellent item of food for anaemics.

 ## Chilli

Red chillies are filled with nutrients like Vitamins A and C besides they contain minor amounts iron, potassium and niacin also.

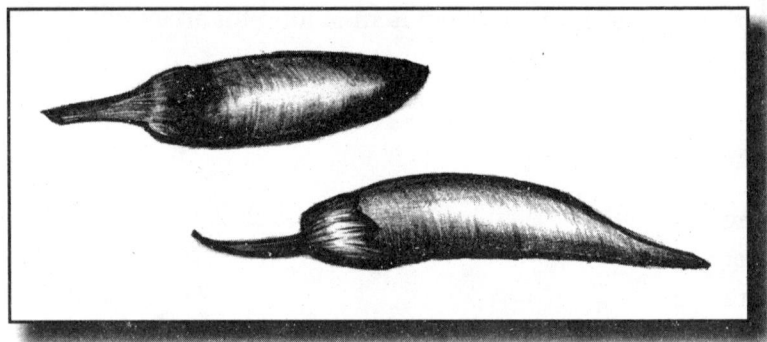

Red chillies or red capsicums should be rushed in water, strained and orange juice and sugar should be added to it. This drink taken twice daily reduces fever. Chillies induce cooling and perspiration. Sugar supplies energy and orange juice supplies Vitamin C and bioflavonoids proportion should be 1 glass orange juice and ¼ teaspoon red chilli paste and 2 tablespoons of sugar.

Chillies also contain pungent elements that will get to the lining of the nose and make it liquid thus opening a stuffy nose and flushing the cold virus out. Chicken soup or dal soup mixed with a teaspoon of chilli powder and drunk piping hot helps in clearing a stuffy nose

Chillies can also boost your mood. They stimulate the pain receptors in the mouth and they release endorphins in the nervous system. Endorphins give a feeling of well-being to the body making one feel on top of the world.

French Beans

French beans are used as food since ancient times. They are natives of America. Although they are low in calories, they are loaded with nutrients like proteins, fats, carbohydrates, fibre, calcium, phosphorus and Vitamins A, B, C and niacin. Their juice stimulates the production of insulin in diabetics. They are an excellent source of Vitamin K which helps to maintain strong bones. They are also good for the prevention of heart disease. They help reduce the frequency and intensity of migraine attacks. Being rich sources of iron, they provide energy to menstruating and pregnant women.

Gooseberry

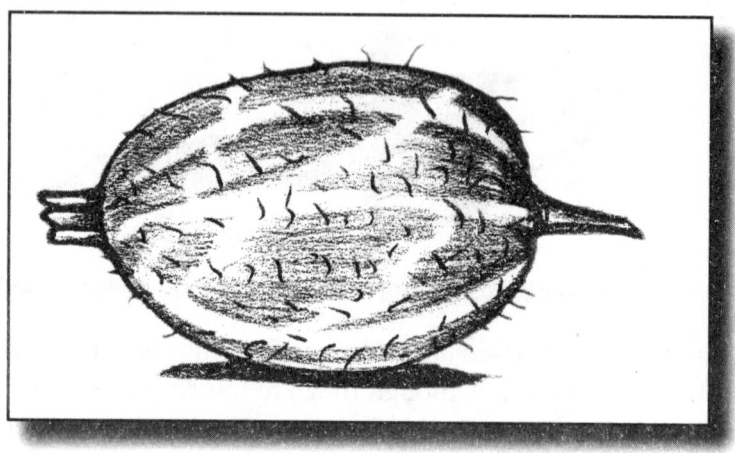

Indian gooseberry is the richest source Vitamin C found in any fruit or vegetable. No other food can stand in comparison with it as a source of medicinal properties. Since it is rich in Vitamin C it produces collagen in the body. Collagen is a glue that holds us and our skin together and stops wrinkling of the skin. Indian gooseberry also provides healthy teeth, skin, eyes and hair. It provides resistance to disease and infection and helps in healing of wounds. It purifies the blood, revitalizes the body and increases semen. It prevents and reduces heartburn. Eating two of these with two almonds in the morning helps balance the digestive juices, prevents acidity and cleanses the intestines. Amla being the best source of Vitamin C boosts immunity and fights cough and common cold.

Kokum

Kokum is a sour dried fruit of the plant gercenia indica. It is commonly found in the tropical rains forests of Mysore and Coorg in south India. The fruit is of pale green colour when raw but becomes deep red in colour when it ripens. It has a sweet and sour taste because it contains malic and citric acids.

Benefits of Kokum

The seeds of the fruit yield kocum butter. Kokum butter is rich in stearic and olasic butter.

It is used as a local application to cure ulcers and cracks in the lips hands and heels of the feet. Kokum butter if applied on the skin cures a dry skin and makes it soft and smooth.

It cures piles, dysentery, tumours and cardiac ailments. A drink made up of kokum syrup and coconut milk is used to cure indigestion.

Kokum drink is used to keep the body cool by beating the relentless heat of the summer and it protects a person against sun stroke. To prepare the drink, soak kokums in water for half an hour. Squeeze out the juice and strain in a fine cloth. Boil for 20 minutes, add sugar and boil for another 20 minutes. Strain and bottle and keep in a cool, dry place or a refrigerator. To serve, dilute the syrup either with chilled water or ice cold soda. Kokums are excellent for reducing sugar in urine. It also removes gases and keeps digestive tract healthy by removing constipation and thereby increasing appetite. This fruit is a powerful antioxidant and it rejuvenates the body and also in improving the functions of the liver cardiovascular system. Kokums also help in reducing obesity and cholesterol. Kokums are full of anti-bacterial and anti-ulcer properties.

Lime

Lime is known as an orange with a sour taste. It is an orange with more acid and less sugar. It is an excellent source of citric acid, natural sugar and Vitamin C. It also contains bioflavonoides, Vitamin P and traces of niacin, thiamine, calcium and phosphorus. It is an extremely rich source of Vitamin C and so, it is excellent for maintaining the health of the skin, teeth and eyes. It checks excessive flow of bile in the stomach and cleanses the mouth. It removes phlegm from the throat and wind from the digestive tract. It helps in the diseases like constipation, throat infection, acidity, rheumatism and intestinal worms.

Lime juice helps in the metabolism of calcium and helps in maintaining healthy teeth and bones. Lemon juice is diuretic and so gives relief in kidney and bladder problems, destroys intestinal worms and cures hepatitis. The Vitamin

P in lemon juice strengthens the blood vessels and prevents internal bleeding. Since lemon juice is rich in potassium, it is useful to patients of hyper tension.

Healing Power of Lime

Constipation: Take in empty stomach a glass of warm water mixed with juice of 1 lime and 1 tablespoon of honey to cure constipation.

Diabetes: Lemon juice mixed in 1 glass of water quenches the thirst in diabetes and helps in dry mouth.

Fever: 1 glass of water mixed with juice of a lime prevents flu, malaria and cold, provides relief in fever and abdominal disorders, calms the nerves and the heart, allays palpitation, and cures scurvey, gout and rheumatism.

Vomiting: Take 1 teaspoon each of lime, tulsi juice and honey. Mix together and take twice everyday to control vomiting.

Body odour: Take 1 tablespoon of the white pulp of lime from its inside. Mix with a cup of water and boil for 5 minutes. Strain and add 3 drops of spirit of camphor and 3 drops of lime juice. Apply on the body every night before going to bed. This will reduce the body odour considerably.

Fever blisters: When you have cold, you get these itching blisters. Just rub the areas a few times a day with lime juice to get relief.

Persistent thirst: Make a cold drink with cold water and one tablespoon full juice of each—tulsi and lime juice. Sweeten with sugar and drink to get relief.

Open pores: To close open pores apply lime juice with a cotton bud on the pores and wash off with plain water after 15 minutes and then splash on chilled rose water.

Tired eyes: Take 4 tablespoons each of lime juice and iced water. Soak cotton pads in this solution and place over closed eyelids. Keep them for 10 minutes.

Yellow teeth: Clean teeth once a week with lime juice to which salt has been added. This mixture not only removes the discoloration but also whitens and brightens the teeth at the same time.

Lice: To remove lice from the head take 2 tablespoons of each of lime and ginger juice. Add ½ teaspoon of pepper powder and massage into the head at night, tie the head with a scarf and next morning take a head bath. Do this once a week to get relief from lice and nits.

Freckles: Grind 2 almonds and mix with white of an egg and half teaspoon of lime juice. Apply on the face and wash off after fifteen minutes with plain water.

Dark elbows: To lighten them cut a lemon into half, squeeze out its juice and rest your elbows in the lemon shells for 10 minutes and then wash off. Do this twice a week.

Black heads: Mix together 1 teaspoon of each—lime juice and cinnamon powder. Apply on the pimples to cure pimples.

Freckles: Mix 1 tablespoon of lime juice with a few drops of almond oil. Apply on the face and wash off with plain water after 20 to 25 minutes.

Discoloured neck: Mix together 1 teaspoon of lime juice and 1 teaspoon of each— milk and cucumber juice. Apply on the neck and remove after 15 minutes with plain water.

Obesity: In 1 glass of warm water put the juice of 1 lime and 2 big pinches of soda bicarbonate. Drink in empty stomach. This not only reduces obesity but also gives relief in constipation and indigestion.

Peptic ulcers are greatly helped by lime juice. Its citric acid has an alkaline reaction on the body. Citric acid together with mineral salts in the juice assists in the absorption of fats.

Lime juice neutralizes the excessive bile produced by the liver. The juice also counteracts the effects of greasy, fat and junk foods on the body and helps greatly by reducing acid formation and gases in the stomach.

Beauty and Lime

Dry lips: Mix 1 teaspoon of melted bees wax with half teaspoon of lime juice and half teaspoon of coconut oil. Mix nicely and put in a bottle. Apply on the lips every night before going to bed to get soft and smooth lips.

Skin tightener: Mix together 2 tablespoons of grated coconut with 1 egg white and 1 teaspoon of each, lime juice and vodka. Add a few drops of tincture of benzoin. Apply on the skin for half an hour and then wash off. This not only tightens the skin, it also reduces greasiness of the skin.

Spotty skin: Mix together 1 tablespoon of yeast powder, half tablespoon of curd, ½ teaspoon each of lime, carrot and orange juice. Apply on the face and remove after fifteen minutes with plain water.

Bleaching the skin: Cut half lemon into shreds, add half cup white wine and 1 teaspoon of sugar. Let this solution stand for 1 day under the light of the moon. Strain and use it on the skin to lighten and brighten it.

Greasy skin: Mix fuller earth with lime juice to form a paste. Apply on the skin and wash off with plain water after 15 minutes.

Soft hands: To maintain soft hands take 1 tablespoon oatmeal powder, 1 tablespoon warm water, 1 teaspoon each of olive oil, lime juice and glycerine massage into the hands and wash off after 15 minutes with plain water.

Anti-wrinkle lotion: Mix together 1 cup of rose water, ½ cup of glycerine and ¼ cup of strained lime juice. Bottle and keep in a cool dry place. Apply on the skin every night before going to bed to have a soft and wrinkle-free skin.

Very oily skin: Squeeze lime juice in a bowl of icy water. Splash over the face and massage the face for 5 minutes and then wash off with plain water.

Dull complexion: Mix half teaspoon of lime juice with 1 teaspoon of cucumber juice and apply on the face. Wash off after fifteen minutes with plain water.

Falling hair: Squeeze out the juice of a lime and mix with ¼ cup of thick coconut milk. Massage into the scalp and wash off with a mild shampoo after an hour. Do this once every week to stop hair fall.

Rough skin: Mix in 1 egg yolk with a few drops each of olive oil and lime juice. Apply on the face when this skin feels tight wash off with plain water.

Dark skin: Mix together one teaspoon of each—lime, cucumber and carrot juice. Apply on the skin and wash off after 20 minutes with plain water.

Blemished skin: Mix together 2 tablespoons pureed prunes with 2 tablespoons of lime juice. Eat half an hour before going to bed. Then drink a glass of water. Do this regularly to clear the skin of its blemishes.

Skin bleach: Take 2 tablespoons of lime juice and mix with 1 tablespoon of ground sugar. Apply on the skin and sit in the mellow sun for fifteen minutes. This will not only bleach your skin but also your hair.

Dull hair: To bring shine in the hair, take 4 tablespoons of lime juice and mix in 1 litre of water. Pour slowly over the hair, massage the head and rinse after a few minutes with plain water.

Facial scrub: Mix 1 tablespoon of honey, lime juice and oatmeal powder. Massage well into the skin to remove dead cells and then wash off with plain tap water.

Pack for the whole body: Mix 2 tablespoons of honey with 1 tablespoon of each—lime juice and olive oil. Mix in a few drops of your favourite perfume. Massage your body with this mixture for half an hour before you take your bath. This will remove the roughness and dryness from the body and make it soft and smooth.

Mushrooms

Mushrooms are an excellent source of antioxidants which protects the human body from free radical damage. Free radical damage destroys the health giving cells in the body and gives rise to many common and uncommon diseases. Antioxidants are tiny soldiers in the body which fight the free radicals thereby keeping the body healthy and strong.

There are about 88,000 varieties of mushrooms in the world, but all of them cannot be used as food because most of them are poisonous.

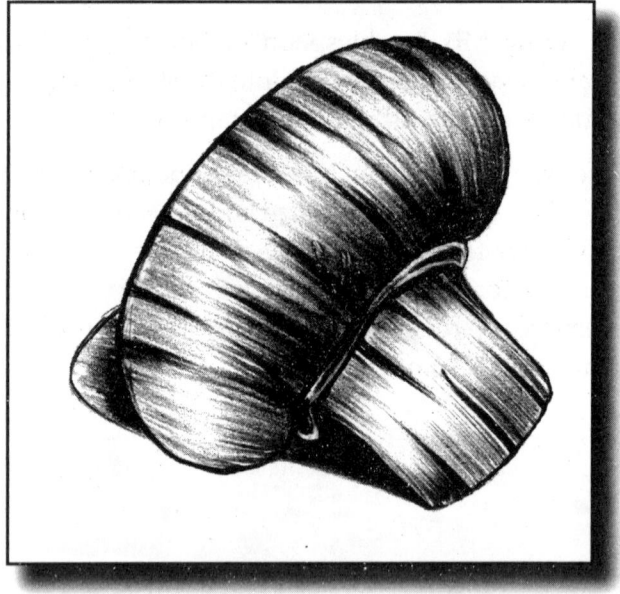

Benefits of Mushrooms

The best mushrooms are white and brown which are known as button mushrooms. They neither come under the category of fruit or vegetables; they are fungus which grow on organic material.

They are a rich source of proteins and therefore they help in combating ageing diseases. They help to improve our immune system and prevent diseases from attacking the body. They make an excellent food for people suffering from cough, cold and asthma.

They decrease the heat in the body and thus keep the body cool. They make an ideal food for the hot summer months. They reduce cholesterol in the blood and so they are ideal for keeping the heart healthy.

Besides button mushrooms, there is another variety of mushrooms called 'itake' mushrooms. These mushrooms contain interferon which is a type of protein which combats diseases like cancer and viral infection. These mushrooms detoxify the body by removing toxins in the blood stream and also improves the circulation of the blood.

The third type of mushrooms are the black mushrooms and are known as 'black tree fungus'. These mushrooms help in coronary heart diseases and also retard the growth of tumours.

These mushrooms contain adenosines which is a blood thinning compound. These black mushrooms are usually eaten by the Chinese which are cooked with onions, garlic and ginger. All of these have blood thinning properties; due to these the Chinese have the lowest heart disease rate in the world!

Onions

Onions contain a phytochemical called quercetin which reduces cholesterol, high blood pressure and heart ailments. Recent studies have shown that people who consume half a raw onion in a salad form, reduces their risk of developing stomach cancer by 50 percent. Onions increase virility and cures insomnia. They are an excellent remedy for piles, blood impurities, tuberculosis, dyspepsia, leprosy and inflammation in the body. They have very effective germicidal properties which kills harmful bacteria in the intestines. They contain a volatile oil which gives relief in respiratory disorders. Onions dislodge phlegm and give relief in coughs and colds. They are beneficial in intestinal disorders and provide relief in indigestion and gas formation.

1 tablespoon onion juice mixed with 1 teaspoon sugar if taken regularly helps in curing piles. To increase virility

take onion juice with honey 2 to 3 times per day.

Eating onions with a dash of lime juice everyday saves a person from sunstrokes and other ill effects of the UV rays. If jaundice patients eat onions morning and night in raw salads, they get relief from this debilitating disease.

Healing Powers of Onions

Diabetes: Special tiny onions if eaten daily in the morning with a pinch of black salt provide relief in this disease. Onions when eaten in a salad provide more benefits to the body then cooked onions. Cooked onions help in the formation of gas and acidity in some persons. White onions provide more benefits than other varieties of onions. Onions lose their Vitamin C content if they are cut and kept for a long time.

Pumpkin

Pumpkin is the largest vegetable available in the world and the best thing about this vegetable is that it can be preserved for 1 whole year! Pumpkin comes in two colours white and golden yellow. It is a rich source of proteins, carbohydrates calcium, phosphorus, iron, Vitamin B and beta carotene. Pumpkin cures acidity and indigestion and helps maintain prostrate gland in a healthy condition. Its juice neutralises the effects of poisons in the body. It provides relief in diabetes, kidney stones and inflammation in the human body. It increases virility. The vegetable is good for maintaining a healthy heart. It controls the secretion of bile. It is diuretic and therefore removes kidney problems. It is laxative in nature and therefore relieves constipation. The orange coloured vegetable contains alpha and beta cartones which stop the cancer from attacking the lungs and stomach.

Sweet Potato

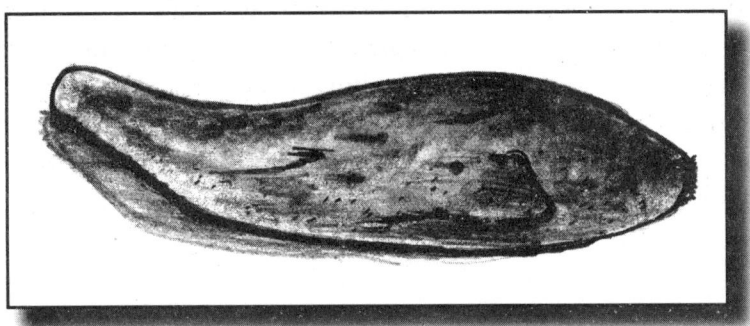

Benefits of Sweet Potato

Sweet potatoes contain lycopene which researchers believe gives protection against cancer and ageing. The orange fleshed variety of sweet potatoes is filled with beta carotens containing 3 mg of this valuable compound in every 10 mg of the vegetable. This vegetable contains 3 times more Vitamin C as compared to a potato. It is a powerful antioxidant which prevents a host of diseases from attacking the body. Since it is a very rich source of antioxidants, it protects the body against falling a victim to cancer. It also reduces and some times prevents plaque build up in the arteries that clog the arteries which help in preventing cardiac diseases. This vegetable is also very diabetic friendly.

Since the vegetable has a high volume of fibre, it keeps constipation at bay. It is also a rich source of potassium, iron and B6; therefore it helps in combating hypertension, anaemia and a host of other diseases. Sweet potatoes contain fair amounts of Vitamin B6. This vitamin is needed by the body to break down homocysteine, which directly damages the walls of the blood vessels. This vegetable helps in the treatment of menstrual disorders and hormonal problems during menopause. Sweet potatoes are high in calories and contain no fat. The vegetable is loaded with immune boosting compounds including beta carotenes which protect the immune system and give it energy to fight against disease causing bacteria, cancer and viral infections. This vegetable is excellent for lowering high cholesterol and sugar in the urine.

Radish

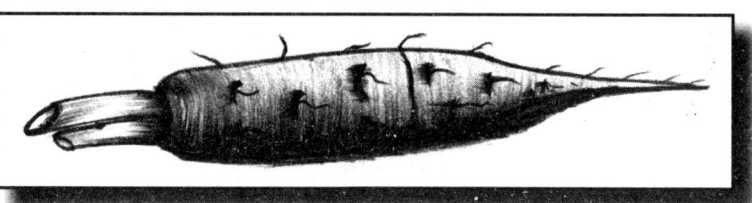

Radish is a root vegetable and grows under ground. There are two varieties—white and red. Radish contains proteins, carbohydrates, calcium, phosphorus, iron and vitamins of magnesium, sodium, arsenic, sulphur and potassium and salicylic acid. Radish is very friendly to the digestive tract and therefore increases the digestive powers of the body. It destroys the hostile bacteria in the intestines. Radish removes burning in the urine and also provides relief in kidney ailments. The tender leaves of radish gives strength to the liver and the heart. Chewing radish leaves regularly cures all the diseases of the gums and teeth and also prevents constipation. Radish is excellent for curing liver disorders. Radishes contain a variety of sulphur based chemicals that increase the flow of bile which helps the body to maintain healthy liver and gall bladder.

Tomato

Tomatoes are actually fruits which are now used as vegetables. They are natives of South America which were later introduced in Europe. The Europeans brought this vegetable to India. Tomatoes are a rich source of Vitamins A, B and C. Besides, they contain a fair amount of other minerals like phosphorus, sulphur, iron, magnesium, sodium and iodine.

Healing Powers of Tomatoes

Diabetics: They are an excellent food for diabetics. Since they contain iron, they help anaemic patients and since it is easily digestible it is quickly absorbed by the body. They also help people who are desirous of losing weight. Tomato juice cleanses the stomach and the intestines and it reduces indigestion and constipation. It provides relief in all types of eye problems. It gives relief in cancer and so patients suffering from this disease are given tomato juice and raw tomato salads. Due to malic acid contained in them they are excellent blood purifiers. Cooked tomatoes as in tomato ketchup, puree and sauce contain lycopene which helps fight lung and prostrate cancers. Tomatoes are excellent food for diabetics and for those who want to lose weight because they are low in carbohydrates. Tomato juice removes indigestion, gas and constipation. It cures eye troubles, weakness and anaemia.

Reducing weight: To reduce weight take the juice of tomato, carrot and cucumber all mixed together. Anaemia drink is a mixed juice of tomato, carrot and spinach which cures anaemia.

Tamarind

Tamarind has its origin in India. It is grown from the tree 'Tamarindus indica' tree. It contains a high percent of sugar though it is not perceived while eating due to its rich tartaric acid which lends it a distinct sour flavour.

Benefits of Tamarind

It is a rich source of carotents, calcium, iron, phosphorus and Vitamin C. If you have lost the taste in your mouth then soak 5 grams of each of tamarind, jaggery, cinnamon, 1/8 teaspoon of peppercorns and cardamoms in $1/4^{th}$ cup warm water for one whole night. Next morning, strain and hold in your mouth for 3 to 4 minutes before swallowing it to stimulate your taste buds and to bring back the taste of food in your mouth. Politice is made of the pulp of kokums to be applied to the swellings on the body to relieve pain and swelling.

Applying the pulp of tamarind to the body before taking bath removes odour from the whole body. Applying tamarind pulp on the face and removing after 15 to 30 minutes cleanses the face of dirt and grime and removes pimples. Tamarind cleans the digestive system because it has laxative qualities. It stimulates salivation thereby aiding in digesting the food. It kills disease producing bacteria in the digestive tract and also prevents the bacteria from multiplying, curing dysentery. Tamarind mixed with salt and eaten during fever acts as an appetizer and improves the taste in the mouth. Tamarind juice stops vomiting due to acidity. It also cures excessive thirst, dizziness and uneasiness in the body. Dried skin powder of the tamarind mixed with curds and eaten twice a day stops blood in the stools. Powdered seeds of tamarind mixed with turmeric powder help diabetics. A paste of seeds applied on scorpion bites removes the poison injected by the scorpion. Paste made of Indian gooseberry and tamarind leaves if applied on sprains and inflammation due to fracture helps in alleviating pain and swelling.

White Gourd

White gourd is a highly known vegetable throughout the length and breadth of India. It contains proteins, calcium, phosphorus and iron. Like bitter gourd, white gourd too grows on vine, but this gourd is sweet in taste. A bitter tasting white gourd should never be eaten as this will give rise to dangerous food poisoning.

Benefits of White Gourd

White gourd has a cooling effect on the body and it not only refreshes it but also rejuvenates it. It is an excellent vegetable for controlling diabetes. White gourd juice mixed with equal quantity of bitter gourd and tomato juice taken in empty stomach on getting up in the morning reduces sugar levels in the blood. A glass of juice of this vegetable given to patients of tuberculosis gives relief in coughing and also helps them to put on weight. Juice of this vegetable if taken by pregnant women is an excellent source of nourishment both—the mother and the baby. 2 tablespoons of juice of white gourd mixed with 1 tablespoon of honey gives relief in case of burning sensation in the throat and the stomach. Steamed gourd seasoned with lime juice, salt and pepper eliminates constipation, acidity and other gastro intestinal problems.

Fish

Tuna is an excellent source of proteins and is rich in nutrients like selenium, magnesium, potassium, Vitamins B1, B6 and niacin. It also contains omega-3 essential fatty acids. Eating tuna thrice a week can lower the risk of death from heart disease for senior citizens above 65 of age. Eating tuna 4 times a week improves the circulation of blood in all parts of the body.

Herring is extremely rich in omega-3 fatty acids, Vitamin D, selenium and Vitamin B12. Herrings are very heart-friendly and also very helpful in reducing sugar in the blood. When buying Herring in cans, buy the ones which are packed in olive oil since this oil is good for your over all health.

Shark liver oil contains high quantities of specific fats like alkylglycerols which plays a powerful role in preventing cancer, influenza and fungal infections. Clinical trials on women ailing from cervical cancer showed that administering sharks liver oil to patients before radiation therapy caused advanced tumour to regress to less advanced stages. Further trials showed that in patients receiving the shark oil before radiation, the count of white blood cells which add in the fight against cancer was higher than the control group and it was found that people given shark liver oil therapy had ten percent high survival rate.

Mackerel, tuna or *sardines* if eaten 2 to 3 times per week cures migraine because they are rich sources of omega-3 fatty acids. These fatty acids lower the production of prostaglandin a hormone like chemical that induces inflammation and causes migraine. These fish mop up the free radicals on the skin and prevents the skin from wrinkling and turning flabby. These acids also keep the body slim and trim.

Oysters: Stimulates the body to increase activity and the desire for sex. Therefore, they make excellent aphrodisiacs. Caviar is the costliest fish in the world. It contains very high amounts of zinc and so they stimulate the formation of testosterone maintaining male functions.

CHAPTER 9

Oil

The unsaturated fats in vegetable oils assists in the assimilations of Vitamins A, D and E which put a glow in your skin, plumps out wrinkles and provides it with a fresh and youthful look. There are many types oils available which have unsaturated fats. The saturated fats which you consume through red meat, dairy products especially ghee that contain cholesterol add to your worries. Vegetable oils contain two natural types of unsaturated fats—PUFA (poly unsaturated fatty acids) and MUFA (monounsaturated fatty acids). Both of these do not contain cholesterol. The total cholesterol in the body is made up of bad cholesterol LDL which is responsible for clogged arteries, heart attacks and strokes. But our body also contains good cholesterol HDL which sucks up excess deposits of bad cholesterol and takes it to the liver for destruction. To keep the body from falling a victim to cardiac diseases you should always select oils containing PUFA and MUFA. They not only lower cholesterol but keep the cholesterol in check. Amongst the oils the best oil is olive oil. This oil contains a very potent anti-oxidant called polyphenols and this helps in controlling blood pressure and cardiac problems. This oil is high in mono unsaturated fatty acids (MUFA) which lowers bad cholesterol and improves the levels of good cholesterol. It is rich in Vitamins A and E and therefore it is a very effective antioxidant. This oil occupies a place of pride in the Mediterranean cuisine and other cuisines of the world because of its flavour, versatility and health benefits.

Benefits of Mustard Oil

Mustard oil is made by crushing the mustard seeds. It's a very healthy oil which is used throughout northern India, Bengal and Bihar, Nepal and Bangladesh for cooking purposes. Mustard oil is a natural preservative. It inhibits the growth of bacteria in food items and so it is used for pickling and preserving food items. Massaging body with mustard oil improves blood circulation and lends a natural glow to the skin. Since it is anti-bacterial it prevents skin diseases when it is applied on the skin externally. Massaging the head with mustard oil not only strengthens the hair but increases their growth. Mustard oil contains both MUFA and PUFA. It also contains both omega-3 and omega-6 fatty acids which have good effects on the human body. This oil is also very rich in antioxidants which are very essential for normal growth and the health of the body.

Benefits of various oils

In cold weather prevent the chapping of the skin by mixing castor oil with half teaspoon rose water and applying on the skin when going to bed in the night. To counteract suntan, mix olive oil with equal quantity of vinegar and apply the mixture an hour before taking your bath. To counteract dry skin, soak a muslin cloth in warm olive oil and cover your face with it after making holes for the eyes and nose and mouth, let it remain for half an hour and then wipe the face with a soft cloth. Let the face remain as it is the whole night. Next morning, wash with warm water and splash on cold water. An anti-wrinkle cream is made by mixing a teaspoon of olive oil with an egg. Apply this on the face and let it remain till the skin gets dry. Then remove it with a piece of cotton-wool dipped in hot water to which a teaspoon of soda bicarbonate has been added.

The best beauty mask can be made by mixing a tablespoon of gram flour with one teaspoon of orange peel powder, one tablespoon of beaten curd and one teaspoon of olive oil. Mix and apply on the face. Wash after 15 minutes. This removes the embarrassing blemishes from the face and makes it soft and glowing.

To improve a dark and dull complexion, mix in a teaspoon of gram flour, a pinch of turmeric powder, a few drops of lime juice and half a teaspoon each of olive oil and milk. Leave the mixture on the skin for half an hour and then wash off with plain water. Improve weak nails by applying olive oil mixed with white iodine on the nails and the base of cuticles everyday. For chapped lips, the best remedy is to massage them daily at bedtime with olive oil. If the skin around your heels has become hard and cracked, scrub the heels with a stiff brush using soap generously. Then, rub them nicely with pumice stone, wash with water, wipe dry and apply mustard oil. To treat rough and dry skin around knees, elbows and heels, massage these areas regularly with a paste made of salt and mustard oil.

In the cold weather take oil bath to prevent your body from becoming rough and dry. Put 2 tablespoons of olive oil in the bath water along with a few drops of your favourite perfume; your skin will turn smooth as silk. For dry rough and itchy skin in cold weather massage the body with mustard oil, sit in the sun for half an hour and then take bath you will be relieved of your skin ailments.

CHAPTER 10

Fruits

Benefits Unlimited

Fruits help improve metabolism in the body because the fibre present in the fruits takes longer to break down. Fruits eaten as a whole are more helpful to the body than fruit juices. Fruits contain fibres which are helpful to the heart but fruit juices stripped of fibre do not give much help to the body. Besides, they should be eaten with their peels and rinds where possible because the peels are richer in vitamins and minerals than the inside flesh.

Fruits provide energy to the body in the form of natural sugars. They are rich sources of vitamins and minerals and provide the most essential item of food and that is indigestible fibre.

The value of fruits was discovered in 1756 when James Lind a surgeon in the British navy found that scurvy the scourge of sailors was cured by eating oranges and lemons. Fruits like pineapples, oranges, berries and melons are a rich source of Vitamin C.

Orange coloured fruits such as mangoes apricots provide Vitamin A carotene fresh berries contain half as much iron as cooked greens and fruits like bananas, mangoes and chickoos are rich sources of Vitamin A. So, they are considered to be the nature's desserts.

Apples

Benefits of Apples

Apples contain flavonoids which help in stalling cancer and heart disease. Besides they are a rich source of carbohydrates, calcium, phosphorus and Vitamin C, E and B. It is said that an apple a day keeps the doctor away. Since they are rich in phosphorus, they help control anaemia and also diarrhoea and constipation. Only cooked apples are good for controlling diarrhoea as the cooking process softens cellulose and therefore it is highly effective in curing diarrhoea. Apple juice is useful in controlling dysentery. 2 red apples eaten at bed time controls constipation. As they are a good source of potassium, they help in alleviating disease of the heart.

Apples eaten with honey are specially good for heart patients; they are also of great value for controlling hypertension and migraine.

Since they produce a diuretic effect on the kidneys and relieve the kidneys by reducing sodium chloride to the minimum, they also reduce sodium level in the tissues.

As the high levels of potassium they contain, apples when sweetened with honey and eaten, help in curing extreme tiredness, lack of concentration, depression and irritability.

Since apples contain uric acid which neutralizes uric acid poisoning, it gives relief to the patients of gout, rheumatism and arthritis. As these diseases are mostly caused by uric acid poisoning, they cure any and every type of headache.

The sugar in an apple is readily absorbed by the blood to instantly provide energy to the body. The malic and tartaric acids found in that apples aid in digestion. They should be cleaned and washed nicely and eaten with their skins because their skin contains more vitamins and minerals than the fruit. Sometimes six times more than the skin, also the elements which gives its colour to the skin has a health promoting effect on the body and without the skin the apples, they lose half of its Vitamin C. Besides, the skin is rich in fibre which helps in reducing constipation. They also reduce the incidents of heart disease besides it reduces cholesterol and also lowers the risk of strokes. Besides, apples being a good source of dietary fibre, help in losing weight.

A component called Quercetin found in apples prevent the growth of prostrate and cancer cells. Also the elements available in the skin of the fruit inhibit the reproduction of the colon cancer cells. The flavonoids contained in the apples reduce the risk of cancer by fifty percent.

People who consume apples on a daily basis reduce the risk of developing respiratory disease because this fruit

Fruits

improves the functioning of the lungs. Even chain smokers can get rid of respiratory diseases by consuming this fruit.

Apples, not only strengthen the heart, liver and kidneys but also provides relief in dysentery, diarrhoea, constipation and a host of other diseases.

Healing Powers of Apples

Headaches: Each and every type of headache can be cured if an apple is eaten with black salt after getting up from bed every morning for seven days continuously.

Heart: A grated apple mixed with 2 teaspoons of honey if eaten regularly keeps the heart healthy and vitalizes the brain, liver and stomach. In the stomach, the fruits work as an appetizer and also improve the quality of the blood. The malic acid contained in this fruit serves as an antiseptic for teeth, stomach and eyes. If taken as the last thing in the night, an apple helps in cleansing the teeth. The slight acid content of the apples exerts an antiseptic influence on the bacteria present in the teeth. Therefore, they are known as natural protectors of teeth and they keep them healthy and strong.

Apples are rich in fibre and so they help regulate the bowels. Eat at least two apples per day and also drink plenty of water to help push the fibre through the digestive tract.

Apples in Delicacies

Besides eating it raw and taking its juice, apples are also used in cooking sweet and savoury dishes.

Cherry

Benefits of Cherries

Cherries are heart shaped ruby red nuggets of good health. They are filled with antioxidants which guard the body against harmful effects of free radicals. They also are a rich source of Vitamin C, potassium and beta carotene.

They are a rich source of pectin which is a soluble fibre known to lower blood cholesterol and therefore it is heart friendly. Cherries remove toxins from the body and help balance fluid and water content in the body. They cleanse the kidneys and also improve the bowel movement and thereby curing constipation.

They have the properties of lowering uric acid and therefore they prevent gout because uric acid is the main cause of gout in the body.

Cherries contain quercetin a flavonoid which has anti-cancerous effect on the human body. Since the fruit is a rich source of potassium it stabilizes the heart beat. It is a low calorie food and therefore it can be enjoyed by everybody. 250 grams of cherries contain only 130 calories. This fruit is also good for diabetics because it has a low glycemic index. Sour cherries have more nutrients than the sweeter varieties.

Cherry in cooking

They make an ideal dessert and can be eaten in a natural form. They are also used in ice creams, sorbets, cakes and biscuits. Crystallized cherries are widely used in sweets and desserts and also as a decorative item for a variety of food items.

Dates

The fruit of the date palm is native to the northern shores of the Persian gulf. It is a very rich and nourishing fruit known as 'phoenix tree' in Greek. It is called khajoor in Sanskrit. Its cultivation dates back to thousands of years and it has also a mention in the holy Koran. It has been enjoined upon the muslims to break the ramzan fast with dates because dates not only refreshes the body but at the same time it provides the body with energy and stamina. The sugar content of a ripe date is eighty percent and the remainder consists of proteins, copper, sulphur, iron magnesium, fluoric acid and Vitamins A, B and D.

Benefits of dates

Dates relieve stress, anxiety and fatigue and acts as a tonic for the brain and nerves. 8 to 10 dates mixed in 1 glass water along with 5 peeled almonds made into a milk shake and taken gives instant energy to the body. If this is taken at bed time it cures even chronic constipation. This also reduces weakness in the body, increases sperm count in men and also sexual desire.

The fruit has a diuretic action and is therefore good for urinary infections. It is a good expectorant and is therefore excellent for curing diseases like cough, asthma tuberculosis and bronchitis.

It reduces giddiness, weakness and dryness of the mouth in cases of low blood sugar or hypoglycemia. Regular use of dates increases weight; therefore it makes an excellent food for people who are thin. If eaten when suffering from cough, the fruit reduces the intensity of cough.

This fruit is called the 'fruit of Gods' because it not only improves the body's immunity system but also provides it with nourishment and rejuvenation.

Dates in Delicacies

It is eaten in its natural form and also made into syrups and wines. It is included in chutneys cakes and desserts. Dry form of dates is used in kheers, payasams (Indian sweet dish), sweets and desserts.

Grapefruit

Grapefruit is related to citrus fruits like oranges, sweet limes and lemons. It is much bigger in size and its flesh is either white, pink or ruby red. Grape fruit is considered to be a cross breed of orange and pomelo, a citrus fruit and it is widely grown in Florida USA. It is a sweet, slightly tangy fruit which has good nutritional benefits for human body.

Grapefruit is a new ammunition in the war against heart disease because it helps in lowering bad cholesterol. Many people having high cholesterol eat excessive carbohydrates. The sugar in these foods is absorbed into the blood stream which causes a sharp rise in the blood sugar. The pancreas have to produce extra insulin to balance the blood sugar which if not checked, this sugar travels to the liver and stimulates bad cholesterol formation. To help prevent this from happening, you have to daily eat fruits like grape fruits which regulate blood sugar and reduce the production of cholesterol.

Grapefruit like all citrus fruits is a rich source of Vitamin C, helps in reducing the symptoms of common cold. It also helps in reducing inflammatory conditions like asthma, osteoarthritis and rheumatoid arthritis.

Healing Powers of Grapefruit

Cancer: It reduces the risk of prostrate cancer and other cancers and reduces the activity of tumour cells because of lycopene a carotenoid which helps in alleviating the cancer cells in the body.

Joint pains: Regular use of grapefruits help in joint pains as in arthritis.

Grapefruit also reduces high cholesterol in the body thus reducing the risk of arteriosclerosis. Since it is very low in calories it does not increase weight and it can be enjoyed both by obese people and diabetics.

Juice of this fruit increases the activity of liver detoxification responsible for eliminating toxins from the body and carcinogenic compounds. It is full of anti-bacterial, anti-viral and anti-inflammatory properties.

Culinary uses

The fruit is eaten like oranges. It can be added to salads, jellies and custard because of its tangy taste. Its juice too is highly rejuvenating to the body.

Grapes

Grapes contain anthocyanins which help prevent heart disease, clot formation and stops tumour growth. They contain sugar in the form of glucose. So, diabetics should take them in very small quantities only about 8 to 10 grapes per day.

Grape juice cures anaemia. 300 ml of grape juice taken everyday reduces anaemia considerably.

Benefits of Grapes

Grapes contain citric, malic and tartaric acids. So, they not only provide relief in constipation and piles but also removes burning sensation in the stomach. They are very good for proper functioning of the kidneys. Grape juice helps combat weakness in the body, dry skin, chronic dysentery, heat and burning sensation in the body. It also improves eyesight and skin giving it a soft and smooth texture.

Grapes contain anti-cancer properties; therefore they help in reducing the growth of cancer cells in the body. 100 ml of grape juice should be taken every two hours from eight in the night. But before starting on the juice diet you should fast for a day which will help cleanse the body of all toxins. The grape juice diet should be started with the consultation of your doctor and it should be continued for 1 week and then the tests should be carried out to find out weather the patient has benefited from it or not. The juice diet should be started after drinking a glass of water. This diet cannot be continued beyond a week and only under the supervision of your doctor. This diet has helped many a cancer patient to combat the disease. The flavonoids contained in the grapes have the compounds quercetin and resveratrol which decrease the risk of cardio vascular diseases.

Grapes increase levels of nitric oxide in the body which helps in reducing blood clots and decreases blood platelet. The grapes also reduce the risk of breast cancer.

Oranges

Oranges contain flavonoids which are potential cancer fighters. This fruit owes its healthy benefits to rich phytochemicals. All the phytochemicals found in the fruit are indispensable to the human body because they present a host of diseases right from common cold to cancer. Although the fruit is a rich source of Vitamin C, the fruit also contains 170 other elements like phenolics, tannin, and carotene besides flavonoids which are all very essential for maintaining a healthy body. The other vitamins and minerals present in the fruit are folic acid, iron, calcium and Vitamins A and B. The white membrane covering the orange is an excellent source of calcium. Therefore, they are very good for the health of the teeth and the bones.

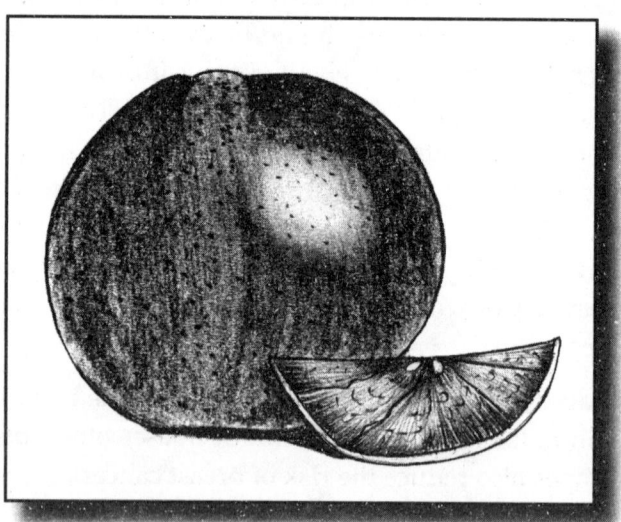

The phenolic compounds present in oranges is known to have potent anti-inflammatory and anti-allergic action on the body. It also reduces the chances of heart disease and cancer and also boosts memory and helps improve learning. So, it is an ideal food for students.

Daily use of oranges helps to improve the immunity system and thus helps fight disease causing bacteria. Its rich Vitamin C content helps protect the gums, prevents bleeding gums and makes the teeth healthy and strong.

The fruit and its juice prevents cancer, removes eczema and other skin diseases and rejuvenates the body.

Culinary Uses

It is mostly enjoyed in its natural form but it is also used for making jams, jellies, sorbets, ice creams, cakes, biscuits, murrabas (Indian sweet) etc.

Oranges and Beauty

Oranges are a rich source of Vitamin C. Its juice or pulp mixed with milk or creamy curds and applied on the face and kept on for 15-20 minutes and then washing off with plain water, makes it an ideal mask for curing dry, flaky and rough skin.

Caution

Do not eat more than two oranges per day. Their high acid content can cause a red rash on the body. The same applies to grape fruits and strawberries. Eat them by all means but never over eat them.

Oranges are citrus fruits and these fruits fight cold and coughs and also counteract diseases like cancer. The new research published in the journal cancer cell supported the general notion that Vitamin C and other antioxidants can slow the growth of tumour, anti-oxidants are nutrients that prevent some of the damage from unstable molecules known as free radicals created when body turns food into energy. Just one orange per day is enough to give the body a day's requirement of Vitamin C. Oranges also contain folate and Vitamin B which looks after the health of the cardiovascular system.

Pear

Pears are the only fruit which is as ancient as the people of stone age because it was discovered by them. The fruit is called the 'Gift of Gods' by the famous writer Homer in his book Odessey. This fruit was considered a great luxury in the court of Louis Xi. Pear is related to the apple family and it tastes as delicious as the apple. There are many varieties of pears ranging in size, colour and taste, depending upon their variety; thin skin is either golden, green, brown or red.

Healing powers of Pears

Constipation: Pears like apples have a laxative effect and so they prevent constipation. One pear a day keeps constipation away. Also, drinking a glass of pear juice per day helps in combating constipation.

Pears are a rich source of Vitamins C, E and copper. Vitamin C is a powerful antioxidant which kills free radicals improving the immune system and it also fights infection and disease causing bacteria in the body, and Vitamin E provides health of the heart and cardiac system and copper protects the body from disease creating free radicals.

Fatigue: Since pear juice has a large amount of fructose and glucose, it is instant energy booster.

Osteoporosis: Pears contain a natural ingredient called boron. Boron helps retain calcium in the body and therefore prevents osteoporosis.

Cooling the body: To keep the body cool in summer, a pear a day is excellent. It will not only cool the body but will also keep throat problems away and soothe a sore throat.

Uses

Pears are mostly eaten as a fruit. Since the peel contains more vitamins and minerals than the fruit itself, it should be eaten along with the fruit. But before eating, the fruit should be washed property.

Pears help the digestive system to function regularly. They are high in fibre and water content. Therefore, they help in preventing and curing constipation.

Plums

Benefits of Plums

There are about 2000 varieties of plums available throughout the world. The skin of the plum varies from purple, red, blue black, green and yellow while its inner flesh comes in varied colours of the rainbow from yellow, green, pink to orange. Dried plums are known as prunes. Plums have a laxative quality in them. So, they help in preventing constipation. They grow healthy tissues in the body because they are a rich source of iron. They improve blood circulation in the body and they help in absorption of iron in the body and thereby preventing anaemia.

Since they are a rich source of Vitamin C they help in preventing cancers, common colds, asthma and arthritis. Plums are very eye friendly. They keep the eyes healthy and strong right upto old age they also prevent muscular degeneration. Plums are very low in calories and so they should be taken without any fear by obese people and diabetics.

Prunes which are plums in a dried form are high in phytonutrients called neochlorogenic and chlorogenic acid. These act as anti-oxidants which kill free radicals.

Culinary Uses

Plums should be eaten as they are with their skins. They can be included into a variety of desserts and other savoury dishes. Since plums contain a harmful substance called oxalates, they should not be consumed by patients with kidney and gall bladder problems.

Peach

Benefits of Peaches

Peach is a golden yellow fruit which is loved by everyone for its juicy taste. Besides its lovely taste it has numerous health benefits. Peaches are an excellent source of Vitamin A which not only gives a smooth and soft skin but is also excellent for eyes, hair and ears. Vitamin A is a powerful antioxidant which kills free radicals and keeps the body in a fit condition.

Since peaches are a rich source of Vitamin A, they put a glow in the complexion.

Peaches have properties of de-worming. They are excellent for removing worms from the intestinal tract. Peaches are fibre rich foods and so they prevent constipation and regularise the bowel movement.

Peaches are an excellent fruit for diabetics as they are not high in natural sugar like bananas, mangoes and chickoos which are taboo to a diabetic.

Peaches are an excellent food for people who are obese as the fruit makes them feel fuller for longer period of time without adding calories to their weight.

Peaches are diuretics. They are an excellent food for patients suffering from rheumatism and gout.

Peaches are excellent for patients of asthma and hypertension.

Uses

Peaches should be eaten with their skins. They also can be used in salads, desserts and a variety of other dishes like murrabas (Indian sweet) and sorbets.

Papaya

Benefits of Papaya

Papaya is a very rich source of antioxidants, minerals and fibre. Papaya contains papain an enzyme that helps digest proteins. The unripe fruit contains enzymes which are used to treat sports injuries and allergies. Christopher Columbus called it 'the fruit of the angels'. Papayas are a rich source of Vitamins C, E and beta carotene — three very powerful antioxidants.

Papaya helps prevent the oxidation of cholesterol. Only when the cholesterol becomes oxidized, it is able to build up a plaque in the arteries that leads to diabetes and heart attacks.

Folic acid found in this fruit converts Homocysteine into benign amino acids. High levels of Homocysteine in the body cause heart attacks by making the blood thick and increasing the risk of blood vessel blockade.

Fibre found in papaya binds the cancer causing toxins in the colon and keep them away from the healthy colon cells. In addition the antioxidants contained in the fruit has been associated with reduced risk of colon cancer.

The enzymes contained in papaya help to lower the inflammation and hasten the healing process in the cases of burns. The anti-oxidants found in papayas help people suffering from asthma, osteoarthritis and rheumatoid arthritis. Papayas also help patients suffering from irritable bowel syndrome. It also helps to give a person a healthy immune system.

It is a healthy fruit which not only helps in curing incurable diseases but also common infections like cough and cold.

The seeds of papaya have a spicy pepper-like flavour and are useful in curing piles and dyspepsia.

Raw papaya juice is very helpful for expelling worms from the digestive tract. It also proves effective in liver troubles and regularizes menstrual flow.

Papaya contains arginine which helps male fertility and fibre necessary for blood coagulation. A poultice of the leaves of the plant is beneficial in neuralgia (nerve pain) and elephantitis.

It is excellent for treating pimples. A paste of raw fruit is applied on pimples and washed off with plain water after

15 minutes. It not only removes pimples but also gives a shine to the face.

Raw papaya should not be eaten by pregnant ladies as this may induce abortion. Since papaya induces heat in the body it should not be eaten during fever and pregnancy.

Uses of Papaya

Papaya can be eaten in its natural form or it can be made into a milkshake in the blender with either milk, water or curd. It can be used in salads and desserts and raw papaya can be made in a dish or a chutney.

Pomegranate

Pomegranate is a native of Persia and Afghanistan where it is used widely in all types of dishes both sweet and savoury. It is said that King Solomon had a whole garden of pomegranates as he was very fond of the delicious fruit.

Benefits of Pomegranate

Pomegranates contain proteins, fat, carbohydrates, calcium, phosphorus iron and Vitamins B2 and C. The fruit is a tonic for the heart and removes pain in the heart. It cures vocal and diseases of the mouth. It allays burning sensation in the stomach. It cures anaemia. It is a very useful fruit for curing dysentery. On account of its astringent properties it gives relief in diarrhoea. The weakness due to repeated motions can be cured by taking 50 ml of pomegranate juice a few times daily.

Dried pomegranate skin if powdered and used for cleaning the teeth whitens and brightens them.

Powder of dried pomegranate skin if dissolved in a cup of warm water and used as a gargle removes bad breath. If 1 cup pomegranate juice is drunk twice daily it regulates menstrual cycle.

If dried pomegranate skin powder made into a paste with milk powder and rose water is applied on the face and left for 20 minutes and then washed off with plain water, it gives a soft glow to the skin.

Musk Melon

This fruit grows on the sandy soil on the river bank. Melons have a golden flesh and they are extremely sweet in taste. Melon is made up of 95 percent water besides having proteins, fats, carbohydrate, calcium, phosphorus, sodium and Vitamins A and C. Melons are a cooling fruit and so they soothe the burning sensation in the stomach. Since they are rich in minerals, they remove acidity and flatulence. Melon juice cures acute eczema and other skin diseases. Melons are diuretic therefore they help alleviate kidney diseases. This fruit also cures constipation

Strawberry

There are about 600 varieties of strawberries in the world. Strawberries were a luxury and therefore were only enjoyed by the rich and the mighty in the 19th century. Today it is enjoyed by everyone rich and poor alike. It remains the world's most popular berry.

Benefits of Strawberries

Strawberries not only have a delicious taste and appearance but also have numerous nutritional benefits. The fruit is rich in Vitamin C, K, potassium and omega-3 fatty acids.

Strawberries are an excellent source of antioxidants. When the body cells use oxygen, they generate by products that cause damage to the body and the result is dreadful diseases. Anti oxidants undo the damage caused by free radicals (free radicals).

Strawberries' unique phenol content makes it a great heart protective fruit and anti-cancer and anti-inflammatory food.

Strawberries give protection against inflammatory polyarthritis which is a form of rheumatoid arthritis involving two or more joints.

Strawberries when cut into half and rubbed on the teeth, removes tartar from the teeth and strengthens and heals the gums. The juice should be allowed to remain on the teeth as long as possible to dissolve the tartar. If you rub the teeth with strawberry daily it whitens and brightens the teeth and keeps the breathy fresh.

The anthocyanins found in strawberries are carotenoids pigments. These pigments are particularly effective against some forms of E-coli and therefore protect the stomach against disease because they have anti-bacterial properties.

The fruit has anti-inflammatory properties and so it proves very soothing to a sore throat

Strawberries can give rise to allergic reactions to the body. They contain goitrogens a naturally occurring substance in certain foods that can interfere with the functioning of thyroid gland. So, patients suffering from the problems of thyroid gland should avoid them. This fruit also contains oxalates. So, if you are suffering from gall bladder problems you should avoid them.

Uses of Strawberries

Strawberries can be eaten in their natural form, but if you spray on them some cream and castor sugar it turns a dish fit for the kings. This fruit is also used in cakes, puddings, ice creams, meringues and sorbets.

Sweet Lime

Sweet lime is an indispensable fruit in every illness. The fruit increases vitality and provides resistance to disease, it is rich in calcium, iron, phosphorus and Vitamins A and C and so it is chock-full of antioxidants which kills free radicals. The juice of this fruit is given in every type of fever because it provides nourishment to the body and normalizes digestion.

It removes indigestion and acidity, cough, gas formation in the body and blood impurities. Above all, it acts as an appetise. It also removes vomiting and nausea.

This fruit plays a crucial role in reducing the oxidative stress through its potent antioxidant properties and so it builds up immunity. The fruit is considered restorative and rejuvenating also.

Uses of sweet lime

The fruit is eaten in its natural form or taken in the form of juice. It is also made into squashes and sorbets.

Watermelon

Watermelon is a cool and energising fruit. It has extremely high water content. Approximately 92 percent of the fruit is made up of water. Watermelon is related to pumpkin, cantaloupes and squash and other fruits that grow on vines on the ground. Originating in Africa, it was first cultivated in Egypt. The fruit was held in such high esteem by the Egyptians that it was buried with the Egyptian kings and princes. In Mediterranean countries it was a prized fruit since water was always short in supply. People depended upon this fruit to quench their thirst in the scorching heat of summer. The juice of this fruit allays thirst and cools the body.

Benefits of Watermelon

It is rich in calcium, phosphorus, iron, niacin and Vitamins B and C. It gives relief in abdominal troubles and soothes the effect of burning sensation in the stomach.

It is beneficial in kidney and bladder disorders and renal dysfunction. It is good for people who want to lose weight. Since ninety percent of the fruit contains water, it fills up the person without adding calories. The fruit is rich in Vitamin B6 which helps in anxiety and panic.

Watermelon contains lycopene which reduces the risk of prostrate cancer and heart disease.

It is an excellent source of Vitamin C and Vitamin A and beta carotene. And so, it is a very powerful antioxidant. Therefore it reduces the risk of both common and uncommon diseases.

Culinary Uses

It is eaten in its natural form and in juice form. It is also made into desserts and ice creams and sorbets. In Russia, wine is made out of the fruit. Its green portions and used to make chutneys and vegetarian dishes.